75

BOOKS BY HARRISON E. SALISBURY

A NEW RUSSIA?   1962

THE NORTHERN PALMYRA AFFAIR   1962

MOSCOW JOURNAL   1961

TO MOSCOW—AND BEYOND   1960

THE SHOOK-UP GENERATION   1959

AMERICAN IN RUSSIA   1955

RUSSIA ON THE WAY   1946

RUSSIA

A NEW YORK TIMES BYLINE BOOK

SOUTHEAST ASIA by TILLMAN DURDIN

AFRICA by WALDEMAR A. NIELSEN

RUSSIA by HARRISON E. SALISBURY

CHINA by HARRY SCHWARTZ

LATIN AMERICA by TAD SZULC

THE MIDDLE EAST by JAY WALZ

NEW YORK TIMES BYLINE BOOKS

FOR CHARLOTTE

CONTENTS

I	What Every Russian Wants	3
II	Czar and Commissar: Brothers Under the Skin	14
III	How the Soviet Union Is Ruled	25
IV	Letting the Genie Out of the Bottle	38
V	From Each According to His Ability . . .	50
VI	How the Steel was Tempered	62
VII	The Soviet "New Wave"	81
VIII	East Is East and West Is West	95
IX	The Many Gospels of Communism	106
X	Whither Russia?	122
	Index	135

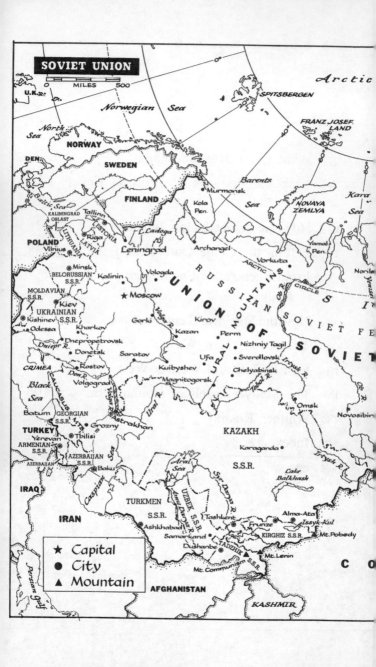

SOVIET UNION

MILES 0 — 500

★ Capital
● City
▲ Mountain

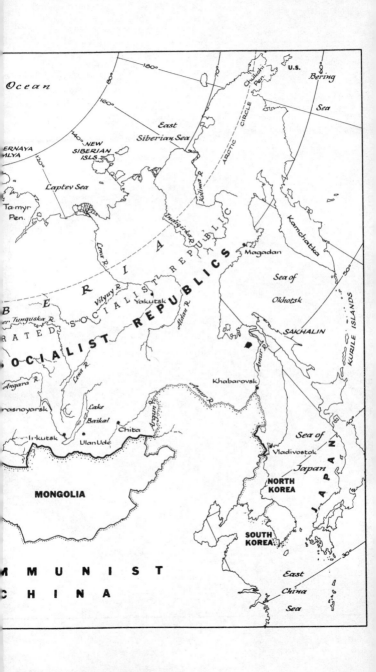

RUSSIA

A NEW YORK TIMES BYLINE BOOK

I

What Every Russian Wants

IT WAS AFTER MIDNIGHT. Across the table sat a Russian officer in stained fieldcoat, his face gray with fatigue, his sheepskin cap pushed back. Wind whistled into the hotel room through a shattered window.

The year was 1944. The place was Odessa, on the Black Sea. We had just arrived after 20 hours in an open truck, lumbering across the endless mud of the Ukraine with the Red Army. The Nazis had fled the city only the day before.

As the officer and I munched black bread and sausage, washed down with hot tea and a shot of vodka, we heard gunfire in the streets and Soviet cavalry clattering over the cobblestones.

Major Rykov was tired but talkative. He had fought all through the war. Three times he had been wounded, and now, with victory in sight, he was looking toward the days of peace, which could not be far distant. His talk was not of the Communist Manifesto or International Revolution. It was of home, family, the comforts of life.

"Perhaps," he said, "you wonder what Russia will be like when the war is over. We Red Army men have had lots of time to think about this question. We are not going to be satisfied with what we had in the past. You may think of us as Communists and revolutionaries. Well, we are human beings as well. We have seen our comrades die. We know that we, too, may die before it is over."

Once the war had been won, he said, he and his fellow soldiers wanted to relax, to enjoy the fruits of victory.

"In the West your life is pleasant and easy," he said. "We don't see why our life can't be like that, too. We made a revolution in 1917 to make things better, not worse. Since then we have sacrificed one generation after another. We have known nothing but hardship. Now we want to live."

I don't know what happened to Major Rykov. I never saw him again after that night in Odessa. Perhaps he did not live to see the war end in 1945.

In the postwar years I was a correspondent in

Moscow. I watched as Stalin imposed harsher and yet more harsh conditions on the people. Each year life grew more grim. I often thought as I watched the Russians, weary, worn and dispirited, of Major Rykov and his dream of better and easier times that would be filled with the good things we know in the West.

The major's dream and that of his generation of Russians splintered on the hard rock of Stalin's insistence on transforming the Soviet Union into a nuclear-rocket military power equal to or superior to the West.

The clash between the aspirations of the people for a better life and the insistence of their rulers on building a powerful state, regardless of human sacrifice, runs through the whole of Russian history. It was true under the Czars. It continues true under the Communists. It lies at the heart of the problems of the post-Khrushchev U.S.S.R.

Lenin laid the foundations of the Soviet state with the resources of middle-class and upper-class Russia, destroying what ease and comfort the country had acquired before World War I. Stalin ruthlessly put the peasantry through the wringer to finance the conversion of Russia into a modern industrial state.

Lenin and Stalin were in the great Russian tradition—a tradition going back as far as Ivan the

Terrible, who in the 16th century crushed the feudal nobility and took their riches to build the Russian monarchy. Peter the Great (1672–1725) sequestered the wealth of the Russian Orthodox Church. He turned the nobility into a "service" class and put the peasants on the path to serfdom—all in the cause of erecting a mightier Russia.

Today the Soviet Union occupies one-sixth of the earth's land surface. It possesses almost every natural resource. Its population of 230 million is one of the world's largest. It stands second to the United States in industry. In recent years it has made startling advances in science, education and technology. It was the first nation to launch a satellite into space, was the first to send a human being into the cosmos and may well be the first to launch an expedition to the moon.

Yet the Soviet Union still lags behind smaller, less powerful European nations in standards of living, conditions of work, productivity of labor, efficiency of factories and the amenities of ordinary existence. Food and housing shortages chronically recur. Automobiles are still luxuries. Women shoppers spend hours in queues waiting for scarce items —or just waiting to be waited on. Only 20 miles outside Moscow one can find log villages, dirt roads, village wells and peasants in cotton-padded jackets and felt *valenki,* or boots, living much as their ancestors lived in the Russia of Peter the Great.

What is the explanation of this paradox? Why can't a state that launches cosmonauts into space provide enough eggs and milk for its city children during the winter months? Why can't a nation capable of producing scientists who unraveled the secret of nuclear power build modern highways into the countryside, where millions of peasants still inhabit what Russians call "bear's corners"?

The answer lies in a tragedy which befell Russia nearly 700 years ago—the effects of which she has not yet overcome despite enormous efforts, ruthless leadership and incalculable toil and privation.

The tragedy was the invasion and subjugation of Russia by the Mongol hordes of the fabulous Genghis Khan early in the 13th century. Genghis died before the country was brought to heel, but his able sons and grandsons overran virtually all of modern Russia, penetrating deep into Central Europe. Though they were quickly pushed out of Central Europe, it was nearly 300 years before the Russians painfully fought their way back to full independence.

Before the Mongol invasion Old Russia, with Kiev as the capital, had been a nation whose culture and achievements rivaled those of France. After the invasion her cities lay in heaps of smoking ruins, her fields were laid waste, mountains of skulls marked the battlegrounds where her men had perished, her women had been driven into slavery and concubinage and her history and tradition almost obliterated.

For more than two centuries the energies of the emerging Russian leadership were perforce concentrated on lifting the Mongol yoke. The Renaissance and the Reformation, which stimulated Western Europe, passed Russia by. Once Ivan the Terrible had finally crushed the Mongol horde, the long struggle to bring Russia up to Europe's level began. Today—nearly 400 years after the death of Ivan—the struggle is still in progress.

It is this struggle that has caused one Russian ruler after another to put guns before butter, to build steel mills instead of fine new apartment houses, to invest in physics laboratories rather than swimming pools, to dig new canals instead of building public parks, to manufacture heavy tanks rather than sports cars.

Early in his long rule Stalin made a speech in which he stated Russia's problem as well as it has ever been put. Addressing his lieutenants in the drive to industrialize the Soviet Union, Stalin said:

"Old Russia . . . was ceaselessly beaten for her backwardness. She was beaten by the Mongol khans. She was beaten by Turkish beys. She was

beaten by Swedish feudal lords. She was beaten by
Polish-Lithuanian *pans*. She was beaten by Anglo-
French capitalists. She was beaten by Japanese
barons.

"She was beaten by all—for her backwardness.
For military backwardness. For cultural backwardness. For political backwardness. For industrial
backwardness. For agricultural backwardness. She
was beaten because to beat her was profitable and
went unpunished.

"We are 50 or 100 years behind the advanced
countries. We must make good this lag in 10 years.
Either we do it or they crush us."

By this philosophy Stalin justified the ruthless
imposition of collective farming, the lowering of
the living standards to subsistence levels to speed
industrialization, the use of force and terror to
whip a sullen populace into ever greater feats of endeavor.

The Soviet Union survived World War II. But
the margin was paper-thin. Instead of giving his
people the relaxation they had hoped for, Stalin
drove them to new herculean efforts: to repair the
fantastic war damage, especially to industry; to re-
sume the task of pushing Russia up to Western
levels economically; to match or exceed Western
technological-military power.

Once again the dreams of Major Rykov and ordinary Russians withered into nothing.

Stalin died on March 5, 1953. His successors—in particular, Nikita S. Khrushchev—tried to have it both ways: to continue the drive for industrial and military superiority, yet to raise living standards and, at long last, began to satisfy some of the longings of the average Russian man and woman.

Premier Khrushchev attempted to tackle the enormous backlog of problems created by Stalin's single-minded effort to propel the Soviet Union in one leap from almost medieval levels to those of the 20th century.

Frankly revealing that Soviet agriculture produced little more in 1952 than was turned out in 1916, the last year of the Czars, Khrushchev tried a dozen expedients. He plowed up and sowed to grain nearly 100 million acres of previously uncultivated lands in Siberia and Kazakhstan. He sharply increased the take-home pay of farmers. He consolidated farms in an effort to improve administration. He campaigned for more productive crops, especially corn. He called for better farm methods, more mechanization, the use of hybrid seed and extensive application of chemical fertilizers and pesticides.

At the same time he made grandiose promises to the people: the Soviet Union would overtake the United States in the production of meat, milk and butter by 1965; Russia's standard of living would equal or exceed that of the United States by 1970 or 1975. He launched programs for new housing in Moscow, Leningrad and other leading cities. He opened new stores and stocked them with a variety of items not seen in many years. Clothing became more abundant. The quality of goods and services rose.

Living conditions did improve, but far less than Khrushchev promised. He faced the same dilemma as his predecessors. He pushed Russia into first place in the space race. He continued to invest heavily in steel and capital-goods industries. Defense spending absorbed huge amounts, particularly for missiles and rockets. He committed big sums to foreign aid for countries like Cuba, Egypt, India and Indonesia.

There just wasn't enough production or money to go around. Khrushchev's farm programs proved no panacea. A crop failure in 1963 compelled him to spend $1 billion to buy wheat from the United States, Canada and Australia. Meat, milk and butter almost vanished from the markets. The standard of living dropped. Khrushchev cut defense spending —and the army generals grumbled. He cut off a huge aid program to China—and reaped a violent ideological quarrel that splintered the Communist world. The spectacular rate of increase in Soviet production sagged violently.

The troubles piled up and up and up. Finally, in October, 1964, Khrushchev was deposed by his associates. Under the new Premier, Aleksei N. Kosygin, and the new Communist party chief, Leonid I. Brezhnev, a fresh start was promised. The new regime loaded all the blame for the U.S.S.R.'s difficulties on Khrushchev and set out to try to succeed where he had failed.

But—despite the remarkable progress and achievements of the Soviet Union—the problem was not much different from that which had confronted Russia's leaders in the past. It was, essentially, how to close the gap which still remained as a heritage from the Mongol despotism, how to give the U.S.S.R. the world leadership and power its size and resources dictated, how to raise over-all production to levels equal to those long since achieved in the West, how to satisfy the aspirations of the people for pleasant, decent living conditions.

Was it possible for any government to achieve all these goals?

It did not seem likely. Moreover, Moscow was confronted with a difficult and dangerous struggle with the Chinese Communists for world leadership of the Communist movement and for dominant influence among the new nations of Africa and Asia and the Middle East. Among the Communist states of Eastern Europe there was discord and dissent. The long-standing problems stemming from the cold war between East and West were as pressing as ever. The question whether the centralized Communist dictation of national policy would ever work efficiently was not answered. Nor was it clear to the Soviet rulers whether it was possible to continue the "liberalization" of intellectual activity and Soviet life which had followed Stalin's death without ultimately undermining the whole system of Communist party dictatorship.

In whatever direction the men of the Kremlin looked they could see problems. The heritage of the 700-year-old Mongol disaster was still very much alive.

II

Czar and Commissar: Brothers Under the Skin

RUSSIA has changed radically since the Bolsheviks under Vladimir Ilyich Lenin seized power on November 7, 1917. But not so radically as the Communists would have you think. There is more continuity in Russian life and Russian problems than either the Soviet regime or its critics often admit. Let me illustrate what I mean:

When I first went to Moscow I was surprised at the number of people in uniform, but I assumed that it was because of the war. When I returned in 1949 uniforms were even more numerous. Everyone wore them—railroad workers, telegraph employes, finance bookkeepers, doctors and even diplomats. The chauffeur who drove my car insisted on a uniform. No mufti for him.

I supposed that it was the Communists who had put Russia into uniform until I chanced to read in an old Baedeker's Guide that nowhere in the world were uniforms more numerous than in the Czar's capital, St. Petersburg.

One of the last great projects of the Stalin era was the construction of a canal to link the Volga and the Don Rivers, thus providing an inland waterway from the Black Sea all the way north to Moscow. It was hailed in Pravda as the "genius conception" of Premier Stalin. But history reveals that Peter the Great had the same idea about 250 years earlier. He began to dig the canal, but had to stop when he ran out of money.

At the end of World War II the Soviet Union established military academies for the army and navy. The uniforms were almost identical with those of the Czarist cadets. The Soviet youngsters were taught ballroom dancing, etiquette and French from manuals based on the imperial curriculum. Some of the elderly instructors who showed the Communist cadets how to bow and take a lady's arm were the same who had taught in old St. Petersburg.

Several years ago I made a long trip into eastern Siberia before the post-Stalin regime liquidated the vast slave-labor empire which had been set up under the aegis of Stalin's secret police. I saw the great camp stockades with their barbed-wire fences and wooden watchtowers in almost every Siberian city. In Irkutsk I visited an old bookshop and purchased a volume telling of life in Siberian exile under the Czars. The pictures of the Czarist stockades were duplicates of those erected by the Communist regime. The chief difference was that Stalin had expanded the prison-camp system to 10 or 20 times its maximum under the imperial order.

When the Bolsheviks, the radical Socialists who formed the Soviet Communist party in 1918, came to power in 1917 they did not dream that nearly 50 years later they would be struggling with the same old problems that had confronted Russia for centuries. Nor did they think they would time and again be utilizing the same means, customs or techniques their predecessors had used.

It is sometimes supposed that Lenin's Bolsheviks came to power through a skillful conspiracy carried out with utmost secrecy and brilliant planning—a plot whereby a handful of bold men seized control of a vast empire without anyone's being aware of what they were up to.

The truth is quite different.

Actually, Lenin and his associates had nothing to do with the real Russian Revolution. They did not plan it. They did not participate in it. They did not foresee it. When it occurred in March, 1917, none of them were even present. Lenin was in Switzerland. Trotsky was in New York. Stalin was in Siberia. The revolution was one of those spontaneous events which occur without anyone's quite knowing how. It was the third year of the devastating World War I. Losses had been stupendous. Mismanagement was beyond belief. Food was short. Suddenly housewives waiting in long queues before the food shops of Petrograd (formerly St. Petersburg and now Leningrad) got sick of it. They began to demonstrate. Workers left their factories to support them. In three or four days the whole city of Petrograd was in the streets. Troops joined the people and the Czar fell.

The absent revolutionaries hurried to the scene and busied themselves trying to take over the provisional government, headed first by Prince Lvov and then by Alcksander F. Kerensky. Finally Lenin, to the surprise of many of his colleagues, managed to turn the trick on November 7, 1917. Stealth and conspiracy had little to do with his success. The coup had been publicly advertised and much commented upon in the press. But the Kerensky government was too decrepit and indecisive to take any effective counteraction.

Once in power, Lenin stepped before the All-Russian Congress of Soviets, meeting in Petrograd in the old Smolny noblewomen's school, and announced: "We will now proceed to construct the Socialist Order!"

The nature of that order, it quickly became apparent, was by no means clear. Not to Lenin nor to any of the men who called themselves Communists.

It is still not very clear nearly a half-century later. In spelling out the nature of the Communist future (to be achieved, supposedly, some time around 1980) Premier Khrushchev in the program he submitted to the 22nd congress of the Communist party described a society which closely resembles that already achieved in the United States —except for the fact that in the Soviet Union industry is owned by the state and agriculture is directly managed (and/or owned) by the Government. He did offer a few variations on the Welfare Society—free lunches in factories, free bus and streetcar transportation. But he put his foot firmly down on automobiles-for-all, as in the United States.

This vagueness about Communist society is not accidental. The Bolsheviks inherited their philosophy from Karl Marx. Marx, a German who settled in London and died more than 30 years before the Russian Revolution, was basically a social and economic critic. He was appalled by the terrible conditions created in England, France and Germany by the industrial revolution. He became convinced that the rising working class, or proletariat, would take power into its hands and correct the abuses by creating an egalitarian society. He offered slogans ("Workers of the World, Unite! You have nothing to lose but your chains" and "From each, according to his abilities; to each, according to his needs"). There would be no classes in this society, no exploitation of man by man, no need for money, no need for wages. The state, as such, "would wither away."

These were fine principles, but they did not tell a Communist much about what to do when and if he came to power. Moreover, Marx was certain that the revolution would come first in the advanced industrial countries of the West, particularly Germany. Russia, he felt, was not yet ready for a workers' revolution. First she must undergo a bourgeois revolution to overthrow the feudal order. Only much later would Russia be ready for a workers' revolution.

Small wonder that Lenin and his group thought their principal task was to hang on long enough to enable the Germans (and other Western Europeans) to carry out revolutions. Thereafter, they supposed, Russia would be able to follow the lead of the advanced Communist regimes of the West.

But the reality proved quite different. The revolutions in the West never came. The Bolsheviks had to make it alone. Quickly they became involved in fierce civil war as the anti-Communist forces sought to overthrow Lenin's Government. Foreign countries, including England, France, Japan and the United States, intervened and fought the Bolsheviks.

In the struggle for survival Lenin never managed to work out any clear-cut Communist system. The Government expropriated the big industries, the banks, the insurance companies and other business and proceeded to run the enterprises itself. The peasants were permitted to seize and farm the landlords' land (contrary to Marxian theory, the peasants had provided the main support for the revolution; if Lenin had tried to interfere with their land-grabbing, they would have quickly overturned him).

Except for a few early experiments, money, pay, profits, inequality in wages and working and living conditions went on without too much change. Lenin never did get around to defining Communism except for one speech in which he said it was "electrification—plus Soviet power," which made it sound something like the Tennessee Valley Authority.

Lenin died in 1924 without working out a careful plan for the Communist State. He had set up a

Communist International in 1919 to try to stimulate revolutions around the world, and up to the last he kept hoping for revolutions abroad. But risings in Germany and Hungary flickered out. Any chance that Asia would go up in flames vanished when Chiang Kai-shek slaughtered his Communist backers in China in a bloody massacre.

With Lenin's death a struggle for power broke out in the Kremlin. On one side was Leon Trotsky, closest associate of Lenin and leading backer of the international revolutionary movement. On the other was Joseph Stalin, a native of the Caucasus, a crafty bureaucrat, a man who believed the future of the Soviet Union rested on concentration on domestic affairs. Stalin won out. Trotsky, exiled, was murdered in Mexico in 1940.

When Stalin started to build "Communism in one country" it quickly developed that his problems and methods were not unlike those of Russia's past rulers. In 1928 many projects for Stalin's first five-year plan for industrialization came straight from the files of the Czarist planning commission of 1915. His orders for "collectivization" of peasants, forcing them into farm cooperatives, and the elimination of kulaks, or richer peasants, were carried out with the mass brutality of an Ivan the Terrible. His purges and paranoid use of terror rivaled those of his tyrant predecessors. His secret police followed Czarist patterns. Like his imperial precursors, Stalin turned Siberia into a vast prison camp. He used forced labor to run mines, fell timber, dig canals and build factories, and enslaved enormous segments of the population to provide an army of workers.

Stalin's phobia led him to bar most foreigners from the Soviet Union and subject those permitted to enter—largely diplomats and correspondents—to every kind of restriction and surveillance. Soviet citizens rarely were allowed to go abroad, except on official missions. Often they were exiled to Siberia merely for having become friendly with a foreigner. Censors read every word before it appeared in print and every letter that went in or out of the country. Almost all reading matter from the West was banned as "subversive."

Stalin justified these measures as necessary to protect the Soviet Union from the "dangers of capitalist encirclement." But anyone with a knowledge of Russia's past was aware that every one of Stalin's repressions had its counterpart in the 19th-century regime of Czar Nicholas I, who even banned sheet music from Western Europe for fear it might contain hidden code messages.

Under Ivan the Terrible and, indeed, as late as the 18th century, foreigners in Moscow were compelled to live in a special quarter of the city under severe restrictions. Travel by foreigners to many parts of Imperial Russia was forbidden or sharply curtailed as late as 1914.

Thus, when Stalin lowered the Iron Curtain over the Soviet Union at the end of World War II it was no new barrier. Rather it was a reimposition of the barriers which had been a Russian tradition for centuries.

After Stalin died in 1953 his heirs tried to put the blame for Soviet isolation and Soviet tyranny upon him. They insisted that by correcting his abuses they would be able to overcome the stultifying and paralyzing effects of his harsh despotism.

For more than 10 years they struggled with the problem under Premier Khrushchev. Then he was ousted and in the indictment lodged against him it was alleged that he had been guilty of many of the same practices as Stalin: personal aggrandizement, rule by whim, dictatorial methods, violation of the norms of law and order, arbitrary decisions, erratic policy.

I have seen Russia under Stalin and I have seen it under Khrushchev. What each successive regime fails to perceive is the continuity of problem and method which runs on from one rule to another, regardless of whether a Czar sits on the throne or a Communist Presidium meets in the Kremlin.

A favorite saying of Europeans about Russians

was: "Scratch a Russian; find a Tartar." The reference was to the long Mongol occupation of Russia. After nearly 50 years of Communism it is becoming more and more clear: "Scratch a Communist; find a Russian." The system and the philosophy of government has changed—at least on paper. But the ways of running the country and the nature of the tasks of the Government vary only a little from one century to another or one ideology to another.

III

How the Soviet Union is Ruled

ONE DAY I was walking down a narrow Moscow street when I came upon a great crowd standing in front of an art store. I pushed my way through to find out what had attracted so much attention and saw a large portrait of Stalin. He was dressed in his marshal's uniform with all his medals.

Nothing was more common in Moscow than portraits of Stalin. I couldn't understand the fuss. Finally a Russian said to me: "Look at Stalin's hair. It's gray!"

"Of course," I replied. "It's been gray for some years. What about it?"

"But don't you see?" the Russian responded. "This is the first time his hair has been shown gray in an official portrait. It has a meaning. It means that Stalin is growing old. It is the first step to prepare us for a change. . . ."

There are two big holidays in Moscow—May Day and November 7th, the anniversary of the Bolshevik Revolution. Traditionally the walls and buildings are decorated with portraits of the Kremlin leaders. Everyone in the city waits breathlessly for the portraits to go up—to see in what order they are hung. For this indicates the political balance of the moment, who is going up, who is going down. It is a kind of barometer of the climate inside the old rose walls of the great Kremlin compound.

Russians learn to read their newspapers in a way different from any other newspaper readers in the world. They learn to look for what is *not* published as well as what *is* published.

Long before Premier Khrushchev denounced Stalin in his famous "secret" speech of February, 1956, the Russians knew that their former ruler had fallen out of favor. During Stalin's life his name often was mentioned 200 or 300 times on page one of *Pravda,* the Soviet Communist party newspaper. A month after his death it had vanished almost entirely.

Even 48 hours before any official confirmation that Premier Khrushchev was in trouble in October, 1964, *Pravda* appeared with hardly a reference to him. Astute Muscovites needed no communiqué to know that their ebullient leader had encountered heavy political weather. When posters for a cosmonaut welcome were put up the next day and the familiar face of Khrushchev was missing, the news was confirmed.

In the Soviet Union the problems of political change are handled secretively and mysteriously, for in the Soviet Union power is vested in what constitutes a cabal or oligarchy with no clear-cut institutional, traditional or constitutional method for transferring or conferring authority.

The fact is that Russia has never had a democratic apparatus. The constitutional underpinnings of the Russian monarchy were primitive. The Czars regarded themselves as despots in which all power was vested. And until the 19th century more often than not a change in rulership was accomplished by intrigue, murder or revolt. An English observer once remarked: "The Throne of England descends by primogeniture; that of Russia by regicide."

Lenin was as firm a believer in concentrated authority as the Czars. He believed in what he called "dictatorship of the proletariat," which meant dictatorship by the Communist party—or, in real fact, dictatorship by the leader of that party.

The Soviet Union has a constitution, filled with fine phraseology, guarantees of free speech, freedom of religion, etc. It has a Parliament, called the Supreme Soviet, which is elected by universal suffrage. The Parliament names a Cabinet and a Premier, approves the budget and passes all legislation. On paper it differs only in detail from the processes of western democracies.

The nation is divided into 15 so-called Constituent or Union Republics, each of which has its own government, capital and legislature, somewhat after the manner of an American state or a Canadian province.

The largest is the Russian Republic, with its capital at Moscow. It embraces almost 6.6 million square miles and its population (as of 1963) is 123.4 million. Second in importance and population is the Ukraine, whose capital is Kiev. Its population is 44.1 million.

The other Union Republics are: Kazakhstan (population 11.3 million), Uzbekistan (9.5 million), Byelorussia (8.4 million), Georgia (4.3 million), Azerbaijan (4.2 million), Moldavia (3.2 million), Lithuania (2.9 million), Kirghizia (2.4 million), Tadjikistan (2.3 million), Latvia (2.2 million), Armenia (2 million), Turkmenia (1.7 million) and Estonia (1.2 million).

Each of these units has its own budget, national language, laws and courts. However, the laws follow closely the Soviet national statutes, and the legislatures in general confine their deliberations to purely local matters.

Two of the republics have special status. These are the Ukraine and Byelorussia. Both are members of the United Nations (along with the Soviet Union itself) under an arrangement dating back to the wartime Big Three conferences. Prime Minister Churchill and President Roosevelt agreed to give votes to these republics to "balance" the votes of the British Commonwealth members in the U.N. As a result of this unusual procedure both the Ukraine and Byelorussia have foreign offices and foreign ministers. Some other republics on the Soviet frontier, such as Uzbekistan, also have foreign ministers. But they conduct no foreign affairs except under the close supervision of the central Foreign Office in Moscow.

Three other Soviet republics have a special status vis-à-vis the United States. They are Estonia, Latvia and Lithuania. These three Baltic states were absorbed by the Soviet Union on the eve of World War II. They had been part of the Czarist empire, but won their independence at the end of World War I. The United States has never recognized their incorporation into the U.S.S.R.

The important difference between the Soviet governmental system and those with which we are familiar is the fact that only one party, the Communist party, is permitted. Only one candidate's name (almost always a Communist) appears on the ballet for each elective post. The Parliament, the Cabinet, the Constitution—all are a façade. The actual power is firmly vested in the party.

There are roughly eight or nine million Communist party members in a total population of 230 million. These members elect their own delegates to the party congress, which is the supreme governing body of the party. The congress names the Central Committee, which in turn names the Presidium (formerly Politburo) and the party secretaries.

But here, too, reality is just the opposite of what is written on paper. Since the time of Stalin the Presidium or Politburo has been the ruling oligarchy. Stalin named his own oligarchy and ruled it with an iron hand. The oligarchy, in turn, named the Central Committee, the party secretaries, the lower party organs and so on right down to the individual party members.

A nation can be ruled by a one-man dictatorship. This has been common enough throughout the world. The difficulty arises when a shift must be made—because of death, because of failure of policy, because of any of the normal hazards of government.

In the United States when the President dies his

place is taken by the Vice President, designated specifically for that purpose. Similar arrangements prevail in other Western countries. The continuity of government is maintained. Authority passes from man to man, smoothly and without crisis. If controversy arises over policy, the difference of opinion is reflected in Congress or Parliament. At the next general election the issue is decided by the people at the ballot box. If they wish a new policy or a new man, they make the change according to law and custom. The decision is accepted as binding.

Not so in the Soviet Union. Lenin set up his Communist party as a conspiratorial organization with paramilitary discipline. Orders came down from the top and were not to be challenged. He permitted debate—often very free debate—before a decision was made. But, once taken, the decision was binding on all. Regardless of reservations, all were required to support it under what he called the principle of "democratic centralism."

Because Lenin himself tolerated fairly wide differences of opinion within the party and was not vindictive to those who disagreed with him, the system did not work too badly so long as he lived. But it was made to order for a cunning manipulator like Stalin who brooked no opposition and no rivals. Under Stalin pure tyranny prevailed. He methodically killed or imprisoned any possible rival or opponent. The mere expression of a differing viewpoint could cost a man his life. As Khrushchev once remarked: "When you were summoned to the Kremlin you did not know whether or not you would come out alive." Stalin encouraged rivalry among his lieutenants and stimulated feuds in a manner reminiscent of the Borgias.

When Stalin died, the stage was set for a struggle for power among his successors. First a triumvirate sought to rule. This was made up of Premier Georgi M. Malenkov, Police Chief Lavrenti P. Beria and Foreign Minister Vyacheslav M. Molotov. It quickly disintegrated. Beria was arrested in June, 1953, by his colleagues and shot in December, 1953. Malenkov was displaced as Premier by Marshal Nikolai A. Bulganin in 1955 and Molotov was ousted as Foreign Minister. Power flowed to Nikita Khrushchev—a man who had not even been mentioned as a possible successor to Stalin, a man who held no official or party post of prominence at the time of Stalin's death.

But Khrushchev proved superior in the deadly game of Kremlin politics. He ousted his rivals and with the aid of Marshal Georgi K. Zhukov turned back an attempt which was made in June, 1957, to depose him through a coup d'état.

The plotters, including Khrushchev's best friend,

Bulganin, had lined up 8 of the 11 votes in the party Presidium against him. When he and Bulganin returned from a brief official trip to Finland, Khrushchev was confronted by a meeting of the Presidium at which he was voted out of office. He refused to accept the decision and demanded a meeting of the Central Committee—a body of about 125 members. Khrushchev's opponents barred the Kremlin to the Khrushchev supporters. But the party chief had an invaluable ally—Zhukov, the Minister of Defense. Zhukov put army planes at the disposal of loyal Khrushchev men and flew them into Moscow. He smuggled them into the Kremlin, and in a dramatic scene Khrushchev turned the tables on his enemies, won the backing of the Central Committee and threw his opponents out of the party.

It was a classic example of the Soviet struggle for power. Once he had won, Khrushchev promptly deposed Marshal Zhukov in October, 1957. If Zhukov was strong enough to save Khrushchev in his hour of need, he was strong enough to oust him, too—if he so desired. Khrushchev was taking no chances.

In reality, Khrushchev's ouster of Zhukov may have been his fatal error. Khrushchev never achieved the kind of iron control possessed by Stalin. He ruled the Kremlin by balancing one faction against another. The threat to him in 1957 arose when a half-dozen different factions joined forces against him. The possibility of another such coalition was always present.

Seven years passed. Khrushchev weathered several serious crises, particularly one which followed the Cuban debacle of November, 1962. When he was forced by President Kennedy to withdraw his missiles he suffered tremendous loss of face. His enemies within the Presidium struck quickly. Khrushchev survived that time. In the autumn of 1963 failure of the Soviet grain crop brought another crisis. But Khrushchev managed to get through that also.

Then, in October, 1964, the bell tolled again. The circumstances were almost exactly those of June, 1957. Once again Khrushchev was out of town, this time at his summer villa on the Black Sea. His chief lieutenants were also out of Moscow. Just as his old friend Bulganin had been at his side on the trip to Finland so, now, his old friend Anastas I. Mikoyan was with him at the villa. A Soviet cosmonaut flight was in progress. Khrushchev talked to the spacemen on a national TV hookup. Nothing could have been more normal, more peaceful. He wished them: *"Do svidaniya"*—"till we meet again." Those were the last words the Soviet public was to hear him speak as Premier.

This time the plotters had profited by the experience of the abortive June, 1957, coup. The lines were laid carefully. A virtually unanimous Presidium vote was assured to oppose Khrushchev. He was kept out of the way until the action had been taken. The Central Committee was primed to act against him—not with him. And, most important, when Khrushchev was finally flown back to Moscow to confront a fait accompli, he could no longer turn to his friend Zhukov. The army this time lined up against, not with, Khrushchev.

The ouster of Khrushchev put into power Aleksei Kosygin as Premier and Leonid Brezhnev as party chief. What sort of men were they? Products of the Soviet system, party men, bureaucrats. Kosygin had managed to survive deadly peril in the last years of the Stalin epoch. He belonged to a Leningrad clique. Every other member of that clique was purged by Stalin. Kosygin survived. Only a man skilled in the dangerous bypaths of Kremlin intrigue could have managed that. Brezhnev is a cautious party wheelhorse who worked close at Khrushchev's side during long years in the Ukraine —patient, plodding, reserved.

By the ouster of Khrushchev did these men become the masters of the Kremlin? Not exactly. When Lenin died, a triumvirate—Trotsky, Kamenev and Zinoviev—came to power. But Stalin ousted them and ruled in his own name. When Stalin died, a triumvirate—Malenkov, Beria and Molotov—came to power. But Beria was executed and Khrushchev thrust Malenkov and Molotov aside.

The Soviet system is not made for collective rule. Power tends to flow into the hands of one able, ruthless man. In the interim between single rulers the struggle goes on. To become master of the Kremlin a man must win the support of all the big power groupings—the army, the secret police, the key party secretaries, the industrial bosses, the important foreign Communist parties.

During the struggle for power, Soviet policy inevitably becomes enmeshed in the intrigue. The dangers are obvious. In a nuclear age they menace the world. Ambitious men in the Kremlin may play politics with intercontinental missiles in order to advance a personal drive for absolute power. They may employ the thunderbolt of nuclear retaliation as a pawn in the game of Communist political chess.

Thoughtful Russians have become increasingly aware of the anachronism of a world superpower's being ruled by the methods of medieval Florentine princes. They have sought to propel the Soviet Union onto the path of constitutionalism, to lay the foundations of orderly succession, to substitute some precept for the primitive law of the jungle still prevailing in the Kremlin.

A little progress has been made. No longer are Soviet statesmen shot when they are removed from office. Malenkov was given a job running a power station in Ust-Kamenogorsk. Molotov was sent to Mongolia as ambassador. Bulganin was given a big state farm to administer. Zhukov was sent to retirement on an estate outside Moscow.

Khrushchev was removed with meticulous regard for at least the forms of the statutes. He was placed in protective custody, but, by Soviet standards, the public recriminations, denunciations and vituperation were mild.

Yet the fatal flaw of the Soviet dictatorship, its inability to handle the succession in orderly fashion, persists. The day may be coming, as some Russians have begun to suggest, when two candidates for a post may be listed on the election ballot. Legalism and constitutionalism may be gaining some ground. But the distance to be covered before the cruel power struggle within the Kremlin is eliminated is vast. Meanwhile Moscow's outmoded system of oligarchy is as dangerous—to the Soviet Union and the world—as it would be to put an Elizabethan coachman at the controls of a modern jetliner.

IV

Letting the Genie Out of the Bottle

ALLEN W. DULLES, who was long head of the United States Central Intelligence Agency, believes that the Soviet system contains within itself the germs of its own dissolution. They are to be found .in the compulsory free Soviet educational system—one of the finest in the world.

This system has produced the magnificent generation of scientists and technologists which has put the Soviet Union in a position of world leadership in many fields, particularly in the development of missiles, rocketry and space exploration.

Can you train a man in the scientific method, train him to subject every premise, every hypothesis to the most critical examination and then set up

a barrier which his scientific skepticism is not supposed to cross? Can a man analyze the infinity of
the universe without subjecting his own system of
government to the same tests? If freedom of in-
quiry is permitted in nuclear physics, can it be forbidden in domestic politics?

Mr. Dulles's answer to these questions is an un-
qualified "No." A man's mind is not made up of
compartments which can be locked and unlocked at
will. Train a man to think, to reason, and he will
apply this ability to every phenomenon in the world
which surrounds him. Education thus is the Trojan
horse of the Soviet system. By educating the populace and training the people to think, the Soviet
leaders have set in motion forces which inevitably
will change and modify the Soviet system and the
Communist method of government.

Already the effects of this process can be seen.
There has been much speculation as to why after
Stalin's death his heirs felt compelled to relax Soviet internal controls. And why did Khrushchev
carry out his dramatic denunciation of Stalin in
1956?

The answer seems to be that Stalin's successors
had no real choice. Dangerous as it was to remove
the lid from the kettle, it had to be removed. The
alternatives were either to let the lid blow off because of pressures generated within the system by

the rapidly growing educated, technology-oriented class or to maintain the strict controls through ever more severe measures, condemning the country to sink into a kind of modern dark ages. If the Soviet Union was to compete with the rest of the world in science, industry and military technology, it had to give the technocrats greater, not lesser, scope. The stultified, repressed talents and energies of the Soviet people had to be released and stimulated.

The genie *had* to be let out of the bottle.

The consequences have been almost revolutionary in terms of Soviet life.

The prison camps in which Stalin incarcerated millions of his people have been closed. The victims of Stalin's injustice have been rehabilitated. If alive, they have been given good jobs. At a Kremlin reception a year or two ago I encountered successively a famous Soviet physicist who had spent several years as a prisoner of Stalin's police, an aircraft designer who had worked for several years in a laboratory staffed entirely by scientist-prisoners, a diplomat who had spent five years in a Siberian labor camp and an editor who had narrowly escaped execution.

Now each was a productive member of Soviet society, honored in his field, invited to prominent public functions, treated as if the past had never been.

The police, who ran the country under Stalin, have been sharply repressed. Many of their chiefs were executed. Their arbitrary conduct was curbed. The rule of the courts and of the law was strengthened. No longer did ordinary Russians fear a midnight knock on the door or the tramp of patrolling policemen on the staircases of apartment buildings, seeking out their victims at three o'clock of a frigid winter's morning.

Workers who had been forbidden to leave their jobs under pain of arrest were permitted to change employment freely. And now they could not be fined or imprisoned for absence or tardiness.

The ban on travel to foreign countries was lifted. Trips to Russia by foreigners were encouraged. In one of Stalin's last years precisely six Americans other than diplomats entered the Soviet Union. Now the total rose as high as 15,000. Russians in substantial numbers began to attend scientific and professional meetings abroad. Cultural contacts expanded. An American exhibition was held in Moscow in 1959 and other international displays followed. Soviet artists began to tour the West. The Bolshoi, Moiseyev and Kirov ballets came to America.

The impact of all this on the closed Communist society was explosive.

Within the Communist world the ice began to

break. The revolutionary uprisings in Warsaw and Budapest in the autumn of 1956 were the direct product of the liberalizing tendencies set in motion by Khrushchev's anti-Stalin speech of February, 1956. The Budapest revolt was smashed. A truce was reached between Moscow and Warsaw. But the evolutionary process within Soviet society did not halt.

With Stalin's terror removed, the Soviet people began to feel free to express themselves. "The important thing," a Russian told me, "is not that we have begun to talk to foreigners. It is that Russians are now speaking to Russians—frankly."

What did the Russians say, now that they talked with each other? They said they were tired of giving up everything, generation after generation, for the future. They said they wanted decent homes to live in; cleaner, brighter factories and offices in which to work; automobiles (like Western Europe and America); longer, more pleasant vacations; a chance to travel abroad; security and a better life for their children.

Their talk, in a word, was much like that of Major Rykov so many years ago in the drafty wartime Odessa hotel.

When these Russians traveled abroad they brought back nylons and lipstick for their wives, hi-fi sets and record players for the teen-agers, washing machines and dryers for their homes. The men bought smartly cut Western clothes (Mr. Khrushchev employed an Italian tailor and wore hand-crafted Italian shoes).

Unable to drive people to work with the lash of the police, as did Stalin, the new Soviet regime sought to stimulate their efforts by providing larger quantities of consumer goods. Soviet washing machines, Soviet refrigerators, Soviet electric irons and vacuum cleaners appeared on the market. Dior was invited to Moscow to spruce up Soviet styles. A few supermarkets, self-service shops and modern department stores were set up.

Under the vigorous direction of Khrushchev's son-in-law, Aleksei I. Adzhubei (since relegated to obscurity), the Soviet press took on a livelier appearance. *Izvestia,* the sober-sided Government newspaper, began to appear with red headlines and jazzy page-one make-up that was copied from mass-circulation London newspapers like the *Daily Express.* Public-opinion polls similar to Dr. Gallup's were started. Columns of advice to the lovelorn blossomed. The press concerned itself with questions of social etiquette. It was even proposed that the prerevolutionary forms of address, such as "Ladies and Gentlemen," be revived alongside the austere "Comrade" and "Citizen" which had been customary since the 1917 Revolution.

Enormous stress was placed on education. Parents, particularly of the working class, saw in education the only safe upward path by which their children might join the increasingly privileged white-collar class. Because the number of places in Soviet higher-educational institutions was limited, great pressures built up for high academic standing. Teachers complained that youngsters were breaking down under the strain of trying to maintain an all-A average. Repeated scandals occurred in which parents with and without influence sought to bribe their child's way into college. There were complaints that cheating in examinations was commonplace.

Despite vigorous efforts to stimulate interest in the Communist party, most Soviet citizens tended to stand aloof from it. They tried to avoid taking up membership if this could be done with tact, and they encouraged their children to enter professions and occupations which would enable them to avoid any special political involvement. This attitude stemmed from the bloody Stalin purges which had fallen most heavily on party members (Khrushchev disclosed that 70 per cent of the Central Committee members of the party elected in 1934 were shot or sent to forced labor).

Milovan Djilas, once No. 2 man in the Yugoslav Communist party, was sent to prison by Marshal

Tito for preaching a theory that Communist Society gives birth to what he called "The New Class" —a class made up of the privileged members of the regime, top party people, the leaders of the armed forces and other important bureaucrats. Djilas said that "The New Class" manifested the typical characteristics of a ruling order—insistence on privilege, status, better mode of life than the rest of the country, a tendency to pass on their position and emoluments to the next generation. Djilas based this theory on firsthand observation of the upper echelon of the Yugoslav Communist party, in which he played a leading role.

Nowhere are Djilas's ideas denounced more roundly than in the Soviet Union. Today, however, the emergence of a powerful new class in Soviet society, made up not only of the political and military élite but also of what might be called the technological élite, is well established.

Kremlin "society" is not just a descriptive term. It exists. The families of top Kremlin officials tend to associate with one another. The children attend special schools. They marry within their "class." A marshal's son is more likely to marry a party leader's daughter than a peasant girl just in from the collective farm.

The new class in the Soviet Union is interested in security, in more comfortable living, in status symbols and in passing on the attributes of superior position to the next generation.

The rise of this class is already exerting a powerful influence on internal policies. Since the class can express its opinions, the makers of policy cannot ignore them. Since the state is dependent upon the goodwill and creative endeavors of the scientists, technocrats and high bureaucrats, it must not only listen to but also attempt to satisfy the demands of the new class, at least in part.

Since the new class seeks, basically, the normal benefits of middle-class life—consumer goods, better living and working conditions, shorter hours, social security, better vacations—this finds a reflection in the policies adopted by Soviet budgetmakers. They must allocate more funds and facilities to providing (symbolic) butter and so have less available for (symbolic) cannon. Whoever heads the Soviet regime, be it Khrushchev or Brezhnev or a successor, does not have the free hand Stalin had in arbitrarily cutting the Soviet populace back to subsistence living in order to finance some new international move.

The influence of the new class on policy goes beyond the question of consumer goods versus nonconsumer goods. There has been a notable lack of popular enthusiasm for Soviet space achievements. "Better learn to feed your people at home before starting to explore the moon," one Russian grumbles. "Space exploration is very nice," a Russian housewife complains, "but I can't buy a saucepan in the store. They say they've run out."

It is sometimes supposed that because of the dictatorial form of Soviet government such popular sentiments play no political role. Man-in-the-street reaction is not as important in the Soviet Union as in the West, but when Khrushchev was ousted his successors repeatedly pointed to the intense dissatisfaction of the public with his spending programs.

This is not the only limitation placed on Soviet policy by the rise of a vigorous middle class with strong middle-class aspirations.

This new class wants security. It is made uncomfortable by talk of violence and vivid revolutionary propaganda. Not only were Muscovites less than enthusiastic about Soviet space spending. They did not cheer the huge Khrushchev-instituted programs of aid to Fidel Castro of Cuba, to India and to some Middle Eastern countries. If there were surplus goods available to help Castro, why not help those at home who needed help just as much? The argument made by these Russians was the mirror image of isolationist arguments against the U.S. foreign aid program. The same logic, the same emotion.

Soviet policy in the competition with Communist

China for leadership of the emerging nations of Asia and Africa is sharply affected by these attitudes within Soviet society. It is difficult for the Kremlin to mount a strong revolutionary program for backward countries in the face of distaste and disinterest on the part of so influential a strata of its own people.

The blueprint for a future Communist Society that Khrushchev drafted for his 22nd party congress in October, 1960, was tailored to meet the aspirations of the rising Soviet middle class. But it contained little that would appeal to Asia, Africa or China. It was dedicated to producing for the Soviet Union—not for some international revolutionary movement—as quickly as possible a living standard comparable to that of the West. It said, in effect, to China, to Africa, to Asia: "We put our own comfort ahead of yours. If you want to reach a level like ours—reach for your own bootstraps."

The great achievements of Soviet technology—particularly in the field of space and exploration of the cosmos—have raised Moscow's prestige to a height never before reached. This has been particularly true in the West and in the United States, where there has even been a tendency to overemphasize the Soviet potential. The feats of the U.S.S.R.'s cosmonauts have resounded in Asia and Africa as well. But Moscow's efforts to capitalize on these successes by extending its diplomatic influence in the backward areas of the world have been negated by the fact, which is more and more obvious to the newly emerging peoples, that the Soviet Union has more in common with the advanced Western nations than with the underdeveloped regions of the earth.

Can the Kremlin put the cork back in the bottle from which the middle-class spirit has emerged? It does not seem likely. The spirit is the product of the transition in Soviet society from primitive subsistence to comparative abundance, from illiteracy to technology. The genie has been released. It will continue to haunt the Kremlin for the foreseeable future.

V

From Each According to
His Ability . . .

IN NEARLY 50 YEARS of experience the Russians
have found that the most difficult thing about living
under Communism is to make the system work: to
make it provide the goods and services people
want, to make it produce the raw materials and
manufactured items that are needed, to keep it
from strangling to death in red tape, to get from
the farms the food necessary to feed the workers, to
get from the factories the things required for every-
day life.

This is just the opposite of what Karl Marx
thought Communism would be like. He saw the
capitalist world as a kind of anarchy which ground
human beings to bits for the profit and convenience

of the few. He thought that if people could plan and direct their economic activity they would quickly create heaven on earth.

It just hasn't worked out that way in the Soviet Union or in any other nation which has tried to make Communism operate. The chief products have been headaches and hardships. Marx and his adherents were dreamers and reformers. They were great critics of the existing order. But they were not very good at foreseeing the practical consequences of the radical changes they advocated.

"Every time I come back from a trip abroad," a Russian diplomat told me recently, "I feel ashamed of what I see in my own country."

The Soviet regime, he pointed out, has been in existence for nearly half a century. Yet in capitalist Western Europe he still finds industrious people working hard and happily at their jobs. They are efficient. The plants that employ them turn out high-quality products which are sold at low competitive prices. The workers live in decent homes. They earn good wages. They have security and good lives. Services are abundant and inexpensive.

"I come back to Russia," the young man said. "What do I see? Sloppy workmen, idling on the job. Poor products, full of flaws. Inconvenience. Bad quality. No pride in work or appearance. Shortages. Inferior style. And all this after nearly 50 years. It's a scandal!"

The biggest problems in the Soviet economy almost from the start have centered on agriculture. Many critics trace the difficulty straight back to Karl Marx, who was a city man. His interests lay in the factory system and the urban proletariat. He paid little attention to the European peasant and farming problems. Many scholars feel he had no basic understanding of these matters. His supporters, particularly in Russia, were largely intellectuals or city workers. Lenin's only contact with the peasantry and farm life came during a year or two of his adolescence spent on a family estate in the Volga region. Trotsky came from the city. Stalin was born in a village in Georgia, in the Caucasus, but his whole adult life was spent in the city.

Lenin at the time of his death in 1924 left farming in Russia almost entirely in the hands of individual peasants. The state operated a few large grain and cattle farms (most of them estates which had been expropriated). There were a handful of cooperative, or "collective," farms. That was all.

Stalin decided to change all this. He had three objectives. First, he wished to break the political power of rural Russia, which could, by simply reducing sown crop areas or by withholding food from the market, bring enormous pressure to bear on the Government. Second, he wanted to extract from the peasants every possible kopek of profit from their production—profit to be utilized in financing industrialization. Third, he thought he could increase farm output by combining the individual peasant plots into larger, better-managed units.

Stalin won his drive to collectivize Soviet agriculture. In a space of less than three years more than 95 per cent of Russian farm lands were incorporated in farm collectives or state farms which were directly operated by the Government. But the price was colossal. Millions of kulaks, or rich peasants, were uprooted and shipped to Siberia. Civil war broke out in some regions. Peasants retaliated against the Kremlin by slaughtering their cattle, burning the harvests, concealing crops from the grain collectors. The toll in lives reached into the millions and many regions were struck by famine. The wounds to agricultural production were so severe that more than 30 years later they are still to be felt. Stalin confessed to Winston Churchill in a wartime conversation that had he to do it over again he never would have attempted the collectivization program.

But two of Stalin's objectives were fulfilled. He did break the political power of the peasants and he did squeeze out of them the funds which he poured into the gigantic industrialization program.

However, in spite of every kind of carrot-and-stick tactic, the stubborn Soviet farmers have never produced at anywhere near normal levels of efficiency.

Even under the diverse program of stimulants applied by Premier Khrushchev the results have been a disappointment. Soviet grain production (except for occasional crop-failure years such as 1963) has risen gradually. Dairy production has grown very slowly. Meat production (except for the private output of individual peasant farmers) has lagged severely.

The problem is intensified for the Soviet Union by the fact that so small a proportion of its vast area is agricultural land. It is estimated, for example, that only about 10 per cent is suitable for farming. And, in fact, in 1960 only about 543 million of the Soviet Union's 5,551 million acres were under the plow. In addition, much of this land is far from first-rate. About 40 per cent of Russian land lies in tundra or marshy northern wastes or is covered by scrubby forests. Much of this region is within the so-called permafrost belt—an area where the soil even in summer thaws only to a depth of a few inches. Other vast stretches are desert or semi-desert or are covered with mountains. The growing season is short. Even in the rich Ukraine (often compared to Iowa) the average number of frost-free days at Kharkov, for instance, is only 151, about the same as at Duluth, Minnesota. Moscow's growing season is like that of northern North Dakota.

In these conditions the Soviet Union must get every possible bushel of production out of her good land if the needs of a rapidly increasing population are to be met. Khrushchev's superoptimistic projections on which he based his boast that the U.S.S.R. would overtake the United States in meat, milk and butter output called for increases of up to 20 per cent a year. Obviously the goals couldn't be met. Actual Soviet agricultural production fluctuates up and down, but shows a long-term growth trend of not more than 2 or 3 per cent a year—not enough for a growing population, a rising standard of living, replenishment of reserves and a surplus for use in foreign aid programs.

Moreover, Soviet farm labor is extraordinarily inefficient. In part this is due to a shortage of modern farm machinery and modern agricultural technology. In part it is due to traditional peasant customs. When a Soviet farm mission visited Iowa in 1955 headed by Vladimir Matzkevich, then and now Agriculture Minister, it estimated the use of Soviet farm labor at a ratio of 100 to one compared to the United States. "By you one man—by us a hundred!" one Soviet official exclaimed in astonishment. Efficiency on Soviet farms has increased somewhat in the last decade, but not vastly.

The inefficiency of Soviet agriculture does more than confront the Kremlin with the constant threat of a food crisis. It hampers industrial growth. The chief labor reserves of the U.S.S.R. exist in the countryside. If they cannot be freed for work in the factories—because of the inefficiency of farming—the over-all growth of the economy is impeded.

The overhanging threat of a food crisis compels Soviet planners to be cautious in expanding the urban labor force for fear that shortages of food will occur in the cities. In fact, this is exactly what began to happen in 1961 when a combination of higher urban purchasing power, population increase and poor production led to a shortage of meat, eggs and butter. In both 1961 and 1962 Moscow housewives found their butcher shops bare or supplied only with sausage and canned meat. Fresh meat was to be had only in the peasant farmers' markets at very high prices. Eggs vanished entirely. Milk was available only for small children and nursing mothers. All this at a time when Khrushchev had promised that the Soviet Union would be "overtaking America" in abundance.

The shortages of 1961 and 1962 intensified in 1963 when drought produced a major Soviet crop failure. Suddenly bread began to vanish from the bakeries. Grocers no longer had flour or groats.

Russian housewives, inured through the long Communist years to the specter of recurrent food shortages, descended on the shops and bought whatever foods there were for sale, hoarding them against a day of even greater shortages.

The Government was compelled to dig into its long-treasured gold reserves to the extent of nearly $1 billion to buy enormous quantities of grain in Canada, Australia and the United States. The grain went not only to feed the Soviet people but also to enable Moscow to meet its commitments to provide supplies to various Eastern European Communist countries and Cuba.

The inability of the Soviet Union to make its farm system work represents the greatest single weakness in the whole Communist set-up. It creates a dangerously haphazard element in national economic planning. Moreover, it constitutes a political handicap of major proportions. Premier Khrushchev, in his bitter rivalry with Peking for leadership of the world Communist movement, based himself squarely on the position of Communism's ability to provide a superior society to that which could be achieved under capitalism. In arguing against Peking's demand for bloody uprisings against capitalist regimes, Khrushchev took the line that when Communism demonstrated that it could provide a better life for the average man, people would naturally flock to the Communist banner. Addressing audiences in Hungary in the spring of 1964, Khrushchev repeatedly spoke in favor of "goulash" Communism. There was nothing wrong, he said, with putting a couple of pieces of meat in the worker's goulash. An empty stomach, he said, was not a good argument for Communism. He referred sarcastically to China's "empty rice bowls." He did not think they provided as good an attraction to Communism as a heaping plate of goulash and a full stomach.

Regardless of the soundness of the Khrushchev goulash formula, he offered it at a time when the bread in the Russian workers' diet was coming from the wheatlands of Saskatchewan and Kansas. The formula was presented at a moment when sarcastic Muscovites were saying that Khrushchev had performed a modern miracle: he was the only man to sow wheat in Kazakhstan and reap it in Canada.

Can Communism solve the agriculture problem? Many critics think not. They reason from more than Soviet experience alone. They point out that nowhere under Communism has an abundant agriculture been created. Most of the Communist countries of Eastern Europe were net exporters of food before World War II. Today, under Communism, each has a farm problem, possibly excepting Bulgaria, which is known as the "market basket" of Communism.

The Bulgars, traditional market gardeners and fruit growers, ship their surplus vegetables and fruits to all the other Communist countries, including the Soviet Union. Yugoslavia, Hungary and Poland have a fairly good food position. But no thanks are due to Communism or collectivism. Yugoslavia imports American wheat almost every year. Most of her agricultural production is still in the hands of individual private farmers, who buy and sell their products and their land just as in Western countries. In Hungary the situation is mixed. The Hungarians imposed forced collectivization just as Stalin did. In the 1956 revolt the peasants took back their land. This action has not been completely reversed in the years since, although there has been intermittent pressure on the farmers to submit. As a matter of expediency the Russians have shipped substantial quantities of food to Hungary since 1956 in order to enable Janos Kadar's Government to win greater popular support.

Poland receives aid from both the United States and the Soviet Union. She is often cited as the one Communist country which has "solved" its agricultural problem. If so, she has done it in curious fashion. About 90 per cent of Poland's farm output is still produced by individual private farmers who own their own land and are free to buy and sell it as they please. This is not exactly a "Communist" solution.

Albania, the most fiercely Communist country in the world, would starve to death in a few months if she had to depend on the output of her 100 per cent collectivized farms. Before 1959 she got an annual grain subsidy from Moscow. Since then it has come from Peking despite China's own formidable food problem.

China has gone further than any other country in attempting to set up a completely Communist system of farming. The Chinese established pure communes in the countryside in which the peasants not only farmed all the land in common but also lived in communal barracks, ate at communal tables from communal bowls, wore identical blue garments and shared every aspect of life in completely egalitarian fashion. It was a Marxian dream come true. But farm production dropped so drastically that China, too, had to enter the international grain market and use her precious foreign exchange to buy wheat from the hated capitalist farmers of Australia, New Zealand and Canada.

In not a single Communist country, then, has it proved possible, where the farming peasant is concerned, to fulfill the Marxian slogan: "From each according to his abilities . . ." Regardless of its successes (and they have been real) in the industrial area, Communism in 50 years has not yet demonstrated that it can handle successfully the fundamental task of mankind: to produce the food needed for survival.

Indeed, three times the Soviet Union survived thanks only to food from America. First, in the post-revolutionary famine of the early nineteen-twenties, when the American Relief Administration under Herbert Hoover saved millions of lives. Second, in World War II and just after, when American food shipments and United Nations Relief and Rehabilitation Agency supplies spared Russia from catastrophe. And, finally, in 1963, when Soviet grain purchases staved off new famine which otherwise would have laid low a nation that ranks No. 2 in the roster of world powers.

As a Soviet observer said at the beginning of 1965: "The revolution is nearly 48 years behind us. Slogans are no longer enough. We are fed up with panaceas. We have got to find a way to make our farms work. Theory is fine. But the only thing which counts is results."

VI

How the Steel was Tempered

IF THERE IS a single achievement generally associated with the Soviet Communist state, it is the transformation of Russia from a backward agrarian nation with a literacy rate of less than 50 per cent into a modern industrial power second only to the United States.

Soviet publicists are never tired of pointing out that in 1913 Imperial Russia ranked No. 4 in Europe in steel and pig-iron production, behind England, Germany and France. In coal she was No. 5 and in electric power she was No. 6. Countries like Canada, Italy and Norway exceeded Russia in power output.

Today Soviet Russia stands first in Europe in all

of these categories. She is first in the world in output of coal, iron ore, sugar, wool textiles and tractors, and No. 2 to the United States in most other major categories.

This is no small achievement. But what Moscow never, never points out is that in the last two or three decades of Czarist rule the Russian economy was expanding at an explosive rate—a higher rate than has been achieved elsewhere except possibly in Japan's period of stormiest growth. In the decade from 1906 to 1916 Russian industry grew at something like 8 to 10 per cent a year. This growth was stimulated by enormous investments by the Czarist Government (state capitalism was well developed in Russia long before the Communists took over)· and by Western European capitalists, who poured more than $1 billion into Russian mines and factories in the period just before the revolution.

Some foreign economists believe that if Russia had remained in the hands of a democratic capitalist-oriented regime instead of falling under control of the Communists in 1917, her economic development in the past several decades would have been even more rapid and spectacular. They point to the tempo of development in Japan as a comparable example, as well as to that in the United States in the last decade of the 19th century and the first two decades of the 20th.

Be that as it may, while Russian production had fallen to near zero levels by the time the Russian civil war was over and Bolshevik control was firmly established in 1921, nevertheless the Soviet Union did inherit considerable industrial resources. Because Russia's industrial development had been so recent and so tempestuous, many of her plants in 1916 were among the most modern in the world. This was true of her steel, textile, metal-processing, chemical and sugar industries.

Moreover, despite Russia's loss of skilled personnel and managers as a result of the revolution (several million middle-class and upper-class Russians fled the country), she had an excellent foundation of technology on which to build. Russia's Academy of Science, founded by Peter the Great, dated back to 1725. Russian universities (there were 12 at the time of the revolution) had been in existence for 200 years. Scientists like Dmitri Mendeleev, who discovered the periodic table of elements, the physicist-chemist Mikhail Lomonosov, the physiologist-psychologist Ivan Pavlov had won world renown.

Thus, when Stalin launched the first of Russia's five-year plans in 1928 he was not exactly starting out to build a house with no foundation. Russia had the natural resources, the basic technology. What was required was capital for heavy investments in machinery, plants and processes plus skill in organizing the new establishments and fitting them into the national economy.

Stalin got most of the needed capital by squeezing down the standard of living of peasants and workers. Planning and organization, then and now, was the most serious problem.

The Soviet Government had abandoned without more than a few very early experiments the idealistic notion that people could be made to work through sheer love of labor or devotion to their country. As the pace of expansion was accelerated it quickly began to adopt many devices used by the hated capitalists.

The Czarist police had often been called out to terrorize factory workers. Stalin used the Communist police for the same purpose, even more effectively. He developed the most pervasive system of espionage and surveillance the world had ever seen. He copied from Western industry time-motion study techniques and the speed-up. Pace-setting workers, called Stakhanovites, were introduced into every production line. The output of these crack workers was then fixed as the norm for the ordinary man or woman. Failure to meet it brought a fine or even imprisonment on charges of sabotage. Workers and managers were shot for faulty production. This was often punished as "treason against the state." The whole of Russia was pervaded with the atmosphere of the worst pre-N.R.A. company town.

Workers were put on piece-rate wages. Competition, or "Socialist emulation" as it was euphemistically called, drove ordinary workmen to the point of exhaustion. Factories were thrown together with no thought for standards of safety or convenience. The accident rate in mills and mines was the highest in the world. If anyone complained, he was shipped to Siberia—to work under even harsher and more hazardous conditions.

The accent was on production, production, production. Factories were assigned output quotas. If they were not met, the managers were shot or sent to prison camp. Each year the quota was raised. The shrewd manager or worker who survived was the one who managed to hold back just enough production potential so that he could meet the new speed-up which was bound to be imposed.

Workers were exhorted in the name of patriotism to increase production. Communist agitators harangued them constantly. Youngsters were enlisted in crash programs to build new mills, new industrial cities, often in the most distant and desolate parts of the country.

As time went on, greater and greater reliance was placed on bonuses. They went to individual workers and to managers. If a factory overfulfilled its production plan by 10 per cent, it received a year-end bonus from the Government which was usually split three ways—one-third to the employes, one-third to the managers and one-third to a factory fund that was supposed to be spent for recreation facilities, medical installations and the like.

Despite these devices—or perhaps because of them—Soviet economic development went forward on an erratic course. Far from being carefully planned, the year's results seldom bore more than the most general resemblance to what had been programmed. To complicate matters, Stalin became convinced that his enemies were undermining the country by deliberate economic sabotage. Year after year he carried out massive purges, sometimes eliminating top leadership levels in industry three or four years in succession. So sweeping were these purges that Khrushchev later contended they had weakened the Soviet Union to the point at which its capacity to resist the Nazi attack in 1941 was seriously impaired.

Viewing this spectacle from afar, Western observers fell into the habit of ridiculing Soviet industrial capacity and the whole psychology of the plan. So obvious were the flaws in the Soviet system that at the end of World War II many conservative analysts believed it would take Moscow 15, 20 or 25 years to duplicate the American feat of creating nuclear weapons. They felt that Soviet industrial, technological and organizational capacity was so limited that the U.S.S.R. would make an A-bomb only with enormous difficulty. Some even thought the Russians would never achieve it.

As a result, when the Soviet Union tested its first A-bomb in 1949 and its first H-bomb in 1953, the West was caught by surprise. Even after official confirmation of these events many Westerners continued to be skeptical of Soviet technical capability. Not until the success of the Soviet sputnik, man's first space satellite, in October, 1957, and subsequent developments in Soviet missile and space science did belated recognition of the potential of the U.S.S.R. come.

Indeed, a countertendency, a tendency to overevaluate Soviet capability, has arisen in many Western quarters as a result of the previous misjudgment and underestimates.

Typical of the tendency to underevaluate Soviet potential was the reception which greeted Stalin's postwar announcement that at the end of three new five-year plans in 1960 Soviet steel production would be lifted to 60 million tons a year. At the time of his announcement steel production, wrecked by the war, had dropped to little more than 10 million tons, compared with a peak of 19 million tons just before World War II.

Stalin's prediction that Soviet steel production would increase six times in 15 years was met with ridicule. Yet, actual Soviet steel production in 1960 reached 65 million tons a year, and by 1965 an annual level of 90 million tons was attained. At this rate the Soviet Union's steel output is capable of exceeding that of the United States in years of restricted American economic activity. U.S. steel capacity now has exceeded 125 million tons, but for some quarterly periods Soviet production has been ahead of ours.

However, in those key indexes of modern technology—oil, natural gas and electric-power generation—the Soviet Union still lags substantially behind the United States, despite sharp increases in recent years. Soviet gas production in 1965 is estimated at less than half that of the United States, oil at less than two-thirds and electric energy at about three-fifths of the American figure. On a per capita basis the disparity is even greater, since the Soviet Union's population is more than 25 per cent greater than that of the United States. The latest estimates are 230 million for the U.S.S.R. and 190 million for the U.S.

So long as Stalin was alive no genuinely effective criticism of Soviet economics and industry was permitted. The fiction was maintained that everything was for the best in the best of all possible worlds.

Any malfunctions or defects were ritualistically attributed to enemies.

In the Khrushchev era the system itself began to be subjected to serious examination. Long-suppressed arguments came to the fore between those who wished to increase consumer-goods output by shifting the heavy emphasis away from capital goods—nonconsumer items destined for use in production—and those who did not.

It was revealed that there existed in the Soviet Union powerful lobbies, representing the steel and heavy-construction industries, closely allied with the army and national defense. This group, christened the "metal eaters" by Khrushchev, insisted on the allocation of more and more funds for expansion of steel mills, metal-processing plants, metallurgical and chemical combines, heavy mining and armaments. They favored production quotas based on weight and volume rather than quality and efficiency. And they strongly opposed the liberalization of working conditions which had ended the quasi-military restrictions on the labor force imposed by Stalin. They found adjustment to the post-Stalin era painful and viewed every effort to shift the basis of the national budget as a direct threat to the entrenched power they had amassed during the long Stalin years. When Khrushchev visited President Eisenhower at Camp David in 1959 he spent a good deal of time complaining about the heavy-industry–armaments lobby in the Soviet Union and the problems it created in trying to balance the Soviet budget—problems which President Eisenhower assured him also existed in the United States.

When Khrushchev sought to introduce new types of agricultural equipment based on models used in the United States, he encountered difficulty. In some cases it took five or six years before factory managers put the new items into production. The reason lay in the fact that the plants were tooled up to produce the old models. Their production quotas were based on the old items. To introduce a new product meant to risk delay, troubles and production bottlenecks. The changeover might easily cost a factory the special bonuses which it received for "plan fulfillment." It might cost a manager his personal bonuses. If production dropped too much, it might cost him his job. It might also cost the Communist party officials in charge of the factory and the industry their jobs. Therefore the tendency was to play it safe and stick with the old. The same fears tended to slow the introduction into Soviet industry of new techniques and new machinery.

It also became apparent that the Soviet planning process was a kind of gigantic game in which the central planning officials pitted their wits against the production managers. The production managers always sought to conceal the true capacity of their plants and the true state of their reserves of materials, since they knew that the plans invariably would demand an increase over what they reported. The situation was so bad that planning officials frankly admitted to foreign economists that they were not able to estimate accurately the true production capacity, output and reserves of Soviet industry.

Because all industry was geared to daily, weekly, monthly and annual plan figures, production assumed a pattern of lags and spurts. The heaviest output occurred toward the end of the day, the end of the week, the end of the month and, especially, the end of the year. Workers, section foremen, managers and industry chiefs strove wildly to "equal and exceed" plan figures before the end of the period. Soviet production figures resembled a fever chart. Under such conditions it became difficult, if not impossible, to coordinate efficiently the complex processes of modern technology.

The erratic nature of the "planned economy" gave rise to a complex of extra-legal operations without which the Soviet system would have ground to a halt. The key figures in making the wheels go round were what were called *tolkachi*, or expediters. The tolkach is a man who can get a harassed factory manager a supply of chrome fittings he needs before the end of the week in order not to miss delivery of an order. The tolkach knows which plant has a surplus of steel pipe that can be obtained—at a price—by another plant which failed to receive the supply it had ordered from a third factory.

The tolkach is not a figure envisaged by Marx for the Communist utopia. He is a private individual. Every transaction he engages in is strictly against Soviet law and custom. He is very highly paid for his services. Plant managers conceal in their budgets reserves for his extraordinary services. Sometimes they even carry a tolkach on the payroll to be certain he will be available at a moment of crisis.

Periodically an inspector or a disgruntled employe or party official makes accusations and a tolkach and factory managers are arrested, tried and sent to prison.

But this happens rarely. There is a community of interest which protects the tolkach. Without him the Soviet system would certainly work even less efficiently than it does.

One of the most serious defects of the Soviet economy is the difficulty of establishing cost-price relationships and of adjusting supply-demand ratios. Under the free-enterprise system these are worked out almost automatically. A manufacturer must keep his costs below the price at which he sells or he will go bankrupt. If he sells one item below cost, he must sell others at a greater profit in order to make up the difference. He must constantly adjust production to demand, for if he turns out goods that do not sell, he will go broke.

The cost-price and supply-demand factors are established under capitalism by the operation of the market economy. They flow naturally and act as a self-regulating mechanism on the production process.

In the Soviet Union the State Planning Commission must set itself up as an artificial market. It must try to forecast in advance what supply and demand will be. It must arbitrarily adjust every cost and every price—thousands upon thousands.

With the passage of years Soviet economists have discovered that this job simply can't be done. For one thing, the Soviet economy is so riddled with special subsidies, artificially high or low prices, that the economists can't figure out what true costs are. In recent times a number of Soviet economic missions have been sent to the West to examine, for example, cost-price factors in the U.S. steel industry. They want to use these figures as a basis for trying to establish accurate cost-price factors in the Soviet steel industry. Agricultural delegations have collected the cost-accounting reports of American farms in an attempt to apply the data to Soviet farms to learn how much it costs to raise a bushel of corn, for instance, in the Ukraine.

The supply-demand ratio has become increasingly important as the Government seeks to increase the flow of consumer goods. So long as every item was in short supply Soviet manufacturers needed to pay little heed to what they produced. For example, for many years the only kind of lampshade on sale in Soviet stores was one made of orange-colored silk. The consumer had no choice. If he needed a lampshade, that was the one he bought. Suddenly other suppliers began offering a variety of new attractive lampshades. The orange-colored ones became a drug on the market. The factory continued to make them and deliver them to the stores. But no one bought them.

So long as Soviet citizens had to wait months to buy a radio they cared little what model they purchased. But once supplies became plentiful, taste and discrimination entered the picture. The consumer favored table sets made in the Baltic states. The heavy, ugly models turned out by Moscow factories piled up in the stores.

In order to discourage consumption of items which were difficult to produce or which competed with military supplies for scarce materials, Soviet authorities artificially fixed prices extremely high, using the price, actually, as a kind of rationing device. This was done with TV sets for many years. Ordinary sets cost the equivalent of $700 or $800. (They have now been reduced to about the U.S. price level.) But such high prices encouraged factories to be careless of costs and production. When prices were cut to normal levels some factories found they could not turn out the sets economically.

The same rationing through price-fixing applies to automobiles. Prices of Soviet cars have always been extremely high because the Government does not wish to allocate enough steel, rubber, aluminum and other materials to put the country onto a motor-vehicle economy. Output of passenger cars is held to low levels. The 1965 over-all production target for trucks and automobiles is in the range of 750,000 to 850,000, of which probably not more than 180,000 will be passenger cars. And of this total possibly 40,000 or 50,000 will be available for sale to private users, the rest being allocated for official purposes.

This means that the ordinary Russian may wait two, three or four years to get a car. Moreover the prices are astronomical. Two or three years ago the Government, by the stroke of a pen, doubled the price of every automobile in the Soviet Union. The result is that a Moskvich, a small car in the Volkswagen or Renault class, costs roughly $3,700. A Volga, which is slightly larger than a Rambler, sells for $6,100. A larger car, called the Chaika or Seagull, is made only for official use. This is a machine in the Buick class.

Khrushchev experimented with several approaches to these chronic economic ills. He tried to decentralize control of industry by breaking up the huge ministries and trusts which directed all enterprises from offices in Moscow. He divided the country into economic regions and put all the enterprises, both industrial and agricultural, in these areas under the control of all-powerful party economic czars.

The idea was that the regional bosses would be closer to the scene and would be able to straighten out production difficulties more effectively. Also, it was hoped, competition between one region and another might lead to better output.

For many reasons the system did not work well. It cut across traditional economic and bureaucratic relationships. Moscow never gave the regions sufficient autonomy to demonstrate their ability to cope with local problems.

When Khrushchev was ousted, one of the first moves of his successors was to abolish the economic regions as well as a dual party set-up under which one set of officials dealt with industrial problems and another with those of agriculture.

Premier Khrushchev's successors turned their attention to an entirely different economic approach that had been tentatively experimented with on a very limited basis under Khrushchev. The approach is called Libermanism after the name of a Kharkov professor, Yevsey G. Liberman, who first advanced the idea.

Libermanism is an effort to introduce into the Soviet system the cost-price, supply-demand features of the capitalist market economy. Liberman proposed that factory managers be given authority to fix prices and determine product mix on a competitive basis—within certain over-all limits.

Thus, if a factory in Sverdlovsk could produce more efficiently than one in Omsk, it would be permitted to undersell the Omsk plant. If this resulted in a shift of orders from Omsk to Sverdlovsk, it would be up to the Omsk manager either to cut costs, produce more efficiently or shift his product mix—turn out more of certain items and less of others—to stay in business.

Instead of each factory's being assigned a target to meet in tons of output and ruble values, the manager would be able to vary his production within the scope of market demand to get the most efficient and valued mix.

Profitability would thus enter the Soviet economic system in a fashion quite similar to that in the West. Production bonuses, salaries, wages, raw-materials purchases would reflect actual market conditions rather than simulated figures prepared by economic planning commissions.

A number of industrial enterprises around the Soviet Union were instructed to run pilot operations on the Liberman plan to see how well it would work in practice. Then, in unveiling the 1965 budget, Premier Kosygin announced a large-scale conversion of consumer-goods factories to Libermanism, and Moscow subsequently disclosed that the system would also be applied to some plants supplying raw materials.

The introduction of Libermanism and the increasing emphasis throughout the Soviet economy on personal incentives, "ruble appeal" (as the Communists call it) and other aspects of the private-enterprise system have aroused speculation that the U.S.S.R. may be edging closer to Western methods and away from those associated with Communism.

There is some truth in this. One of the jokes which was circulated in Moscow after Khrushchev's fall went like this: Khrushchev, in an effort to find out why he was thrown out of office, visits the tomb of Lenin and asks him. Lenin answers: "I took a Russia filled with bourgeoisie and capitalists and turned them all into Communists. You took a Russia filled with Communists and turned them into capitalists."

In the competition between Moscow and Peking for leadership of the world Communist movement the Chinese have accused the Russians of abandoning Communist principles, of putting domestic comfort ahead of the revolutionary cause, of substituting bourgeois ideals for Marxian goals.

The argument has not been without effect. However, the image of Russia as a backward nation which has been able through application of Communist principles to build itself up to a first-class military and industrial power still carries enormous weight in Asia and Africa. Regardless of the flaws in the Soviet system, many citizens of new countries look upon the U.S.S.R. as an example of lifting oneself up from poverty and privation by skillful organization of national resources according to Marxian principles.

Each of the formerly colonial countries is eager to industrialize at full speed. Communism is the only system which seems to them to offer this possibility. Thus, regardless of Chinese propaganda and of Soviet changes in its own system, delegations from the fledgling nations continue to make their way to Moscow, seeking to learn how Russia succeeded in transforming her primitive economy into one of the world's greatest, hunting the answer of how the Russian steel was tempered.

VII

The Soviet "New Wave"

TOWARD THE END of 1964 the Communist Youth newspaper in Moscow, *Komsomolskaya Pravda,* published a selection of letters it had received from young men who put themselves on record against the "uncles." The "uncles" in Soviet terminology are the Older Generation, the authorities, the Establishment.

The point of the letters was that if the "uncles" should call on the young men to make war against the G.I.'s, they would not take up arms. The young Russians said they had nothing against the Americans, no reason to fight. They said they wanted to live in peace with their young counterparts on the other side of the ocean.

The Communist newspaper did not publish these letters to praise them or to spread sentiments of pacifism and brotherhood. It published the letters as a springboard for an attack, as a platform for presenting a moralistic editorial on Soviet patriotism.

What the letters actually showed was how far Soviet youth has come from the concept of the "ideal Soviet man" so often written about in *Pravda* —the product of Communist education and Soviet society, utterly dedicated to the causes set before him by the Kremlin leadership, upright, stern, industrious, disciplined, educated, trained, ready for any sacrifice in the name of the Fatherland or Lenin.

The reality, as every visitor to Russia quickly discovers, is something entirely different. The Soviet younger generation has its eyes riveted on the West. It is bored to death with the "uncles." Its attitude toward its elders is like that of the rebellious younger generation pictured by Turgenev in *Fathers and Sons*.

This posture infuriates the Communist party leaders. Khrushchev denounced the idea that Soviet young people did not look to their seniors for leadership. He said there was no "crisis of generations" in the U.S.S.R. At the same time his censors suppressed a brilliant Soviet film in which a youth turns to the ghost of his father (killed in World War II) for aid and advice and is rebuffed with the savage line: "How can I possibly help you? I was younger than you when they killed me." Party propagandists said it was unthinkable that one Soviet generation would not extend a helping hand to another.

But the fact is that Soviet young people have revolted. They find their country *"skuchno,"* or boring. They pester American tourists for the latest pop records. As fast as they can learn the twist, the monkey or the frug they throw themselves into the new dance, usually increasing its tempo. They refuse to listen to the Moscow radio. Their receivers are constantly tuned to the Voice of America's jazz and pop programs or to similar transmissions from the B.B.C. and Radio Berlin.

English is their second language. Most of them have studied it in school (at any given moment about 12 million Soviet children are studying English). They have invented a slang in which English words are substituted for Russian equivalents. The "in" youngster calls Gorky Street, the principal street in Moscow, "Brodvay." He speaks of his "girl friend." Sometimes he gets it backward and refers to her as his "friend girl." He calls his pal Ivan "John." His sweetheart, Anya, becomes "Marilyn" or "Brigitte," depending on his favorite Western actress.

These youngsters spend a fortune (usually their fathers'—many of them come from the élite) dressing themselves in what they fondly believe is the latest Western mode. They risk imprisonment and even the death penalty to acquire dollars from tourists on the black market. Then they give the foreign funds to Russians who are going on official missions to Paris or New York with detailed shopping lists: the newest in patterned hose, discothèque dresses, mod and yé-yé fashions. The girls "tease" their hair like their Western sisters.

The dream of such young people is a car—preferably something big, splashed with chrome and roaring with horsepower. Many of them have memorized the names of all the well-known American cars. When tourists drive Pontiacs or Lincolns into Moscow the automobiles are surrounded by crowds of admiring fans, most of whom know more about a car's specifications than the American owner. Yet they never tire of asking: "How much does it cost? How far does it go on a gallon of gasoline? What is its speed? Horsepower?"

More energetic young men have formed sports-car clubs. The Soviet Union does not produce any sports cars. But the young men acquire old Moskvich or Pobeda cars, cut down the bodies, soup up the engines, fit them with plastic or sheetmetal bodies copied from Western models and compete in impromptu rallies and drag racing.

Other youngsters alienated from the Communist world sink into delinquency and drunkenness. Despite special youth patrols which comb the streets and cafés during the evening hours, drunkenness is a chronic youth problem in every Russian city. Khrushchev mounted an impressive campaign to cut drinking. He put restrictions on the sale of hard liquor (no more than 100 grams per restaurant customer—about two-thirds of a water glass). He closed restaurants at midnight and shut down most of the sidewalk bars and quick-drink stands. This hardly put a dent in the drinking problem. He had scarcely been displaced as Premier before the new regime gave orders to extend restaurant closing hours and liberalize drinking restrictions.

The real cause of widespread drinking, many Russians are convinced, is simply boredom, lack of amusement facilities, inadequate recreation opportunities, overcrowded housing which drives young people to the streets and bars. Despite improvements in housing in recent years, hundreds of thousands of families still live in single rooms often occupied by four and five people. If a young couple has a date, the only place to go is the street, the park or a bar. Young people do not generally have cars. There is no privacy in their overcrowded rooms.

Delinquency, street gangs, petty crime, senseless attacks on individuals and property—all of the manifestations of adolescent disturbance so common in the West—are to be found in intensified form in the Soviet Union. The problem is made worse by official insistence that "delinquency does not exist in the Soviet Union."

The alienation of Soviet youth from conventional Soviet aspirations and goals finds expression in a higher form in the activities of young writers, poets, artists, musicians, sculptors, playwrights and those whom Russians call the intelligentsia.

It is this class that has produced individuals whose names are now well known in the West. A poet like Yevgeny Yevtushenko, for instance. He is the author of "Babi Yar," a famous poem denouncing anti-Semitism in Russia. The name Babi Yar derives from a ravine near Kiev where the Nazis slaughtered 40,000 Jews during World War II. He also wrote a verse entitled "Stalin's Heirs" which warned that men who would like to reimpose Stalin's methods were still to be found not far from the Kremlin and might, at any time vigilance was relaxed, seize power once again.

These poems were published with Premier Khrushchev's personal approval. However, when

Yevtushenko visited the West in the winter of 1962–1963 and published in France what he called his "Precocious Autobiography," commenting sharply on many of the fundamentals of Soviet life, Khrushchev turned on him and subjected him to savage criticism. With Khrushchev's fall Yevtushenko, who had spent much of the interim in his native eastern Siberia, returned to the Moscow scene and scored a great success with a new daring poem which was set to music by Dmitri Shostakovich.

Another of the Soviet Union's angry young men is Andrei Voznesensky, whom many critics regard as superior to Yevtushenko. Not only have his poems satirized the Kremlin establishment, but after a trip to America he wrote verses treating the United States in very favorable fashion.

There are many more brilliant young people in this category—including Bulat Okudzhava, who recites his poems to the strumming of a guitar in Greenwich Village style, and Bella Akhmadullina, divorced wife of Yevtushenko, considered one of the finest lyric poets of this century in Russia.

A half-dozen major short-story writers have appeared, dedicated to the task of writing about the Soviet Union that exists—not the parlor portrait version of the party propagandists.

There is Aleksandr Yashin, whose stories portray the brutality, ignorance and superstition of life in Russian villages (under the Soviet). There is Viktor Nekrasov, whose realism is reminiscent of Sherwood Anderson's and who wrote a notably even-tempered and accurate travel memoir of a trip to Italy and the United States. There is Vasily Aksyonov, whose *Ticket to the Stars* captures the life and adventures of a group of young people, members of the Soviet "lost generation," in the words of their own far-out slang. There is Yuri Kazakov, whose works have been compared with those of Hemingway and Chekhov.

These are young people of spirit. Yevtushenko had the courage to talk back to Khrushchev himself when the Premier sought to silence him on the subject of Soviet anti-Semitism. He publicly rebuked Khrushchev when the Premier suggested that the faults of some writers could be corrected "only by the grave."

None of these young people is willing to write to order, as the Communist party demands. None is willing to recognize the dictates of "Socialist realism"—the party doctrine which decrees that the test of a piece of writing or a painting is the good it does for the party cause.

All of them have been denounced by party critics —most of them by Khrushchev himself in a violent campaign he conducted in 1963. They have, in many cases, made pro forma statements thanking their critics and promising to do better in the future. But not one has wavered from his creed that a creative artist must first satisfy his own conscience if his work is to have any validity.

The appearance of a pleiades of brilliant young writers and poets is no accident. It is the direct result of the loosening of manacles with which Stalin had fettered Soviet creativity. Russia on the eve of the revolution and for nearly a century before had burst with talent in every field. In literature there were Pushkin, Lermontov, Gogol, Tolstoy, Turgenev, Chekhov and Gorky. In music there were Tchaikovsky, Scriabin, Mussorgsky and Rimsky-Korsakov. In the ballet there were Stravinsky, Bakst, Nijinsky, Pavlova, Fokine. In painting there were Kandinsky, Malevich, Chagall, Tatlin and Mashkov.

The tradition and the capabilities were there. All that was needed was opportunity. Encouragement came from members of the older generation who had managed to outlive Stalin. They included Boris Pasternak, whose bravery and talent inspired many of the new young poets; Ilya Ehrenburg, who dedicated himself to the task of rehabilitating the reputations of Soviet artists slandered and executed by Stalin and who exhorted his young colleagues that their first duty was to be true to themselves; Aleksandr Tvardovsky, who edited the literary magazine *Novy Mir* (New World), which found room to publish most of the new young authors; Konstantin Paustovsky, a venerable writer who made his task the defense of the bright new writers from propaganda assaults by hard-line party bureaucrats.

Others busied themselves re-establishing bonds with the West. They arranged for the presentation in Soviet theaters of plays by Arthur Miller and J. B. Priestley. They revived satires by the Soviet poet Mayakovsky which had long been suppressed by Stalin. They introduced to Soviet audiences such writers as J. D. Salinger, John Cheever and John Updike and resumed the publication of Hemingway, Faulkner and Saroyan.

Nowhere was the spirit of revolt stronger than in the field of art. Soviet painting and sculpture had been dominated for 25 years by calendar-style works, many dedicated to Stalin and almost all keyed in some way to production drives or propaganda campaigns.

Now a fresh wind blew in from the West. Through exhibitions of American modernists, French Impressionists, Yugoslav and Polish abstractionists the young Soviet artists learned of the new world of color and style that had grown up in the long years in which they were cut off from contact. They rushed to imitate it and collided full force with the recalcitrant Communist party bureaucracy. Khrushchev denounced Ernst Neizvestny, probably the most brilliant sculptor in Russia, and other members of the Soviet New Wave in art as "donkeys, pederasts, jackasses, hypocrites." He proposed that one painter be ordered to take down his pants and sit on a clump of nettles until he understood his mistakes. Another, he said, was fit only to paint pictures on urinals. He offered other young artists visas to emigrate abroad and forecast that they would quickly fail in the free world.

Despite violent denunciation, the artists have stuck to their guns. With Khrushchev's removal they have again begun to exhibit their works, showing their close artistic and inspirational connection with the West.

Among both intellectual and nonintellectual young people there has been a tendency to new interest in religion. For nearly half a century the Communists have been preaching atheism and attempting to eliminate formal religion in the U.S.S.R. The effort has conspicuously failed.

About five years ago, noting the vigor of the Russian Orthodox Church as well as other faiths, the Communist party mounted a new campaign against religious belief. Despite this drive, it is estimated that the Orthodox Church still has about

50 million Soviet communicants. The Russian Baptist Church has been singled out for special repressions because of the large numbers of young people, including many members of the Young Communist movement, who have joined in recent years. Nonetheless, the Baptists continue to grow.

Because many young people wish to be married in the Orthodox Church, attracted by the beauty of the ceremony if nothing else, the party has begun to set up "wedding places" in big cities. There a Communist-style wedding, complete with white bridal gown and a master of ceremonies in white tie and tails, can be staged for a nominal fee.

The Jewish religion has been a special target of the party drive. Synagogues have been closed, rabbis arrested, members of Jewish congregations intimidated and sometimes physically attacked. Especially in the Ukraine, a hotbed of anti-Semitism under the Czars, there has been noted a revival of anti-Semitism, often encouraged by official party propaganda publications.

Yevtushenko's poem "Babi Yar" was a reaction against this deep and pernicious anti-Semitic current in Soviet life. Many observers believe that Khrushchev himself was a source of it. While Khrushchev heatedly denied any anti-Semitic feelings, he often told anti-Semitic jokes. He spent his boyhood and young manhood in an area of the

Ukraine notorious for anti-Semitism.

In a reaction against the newly revived anti-religious activities of the party, many of the young intelligentsia have demonstrated their antagonism by public churchgoing. They often attend mass in the Russian Orthodox Church and make a special point of going to Jewish religious services at the few remaining synagogues which are open. Young intellectuals of Jewish background attend Yiddish concerts and recitals, even though they do not understand the language, as a gesture of solidarity with the older Jewish generation.

There have been repeated suggestions by Soviet officials that various anti-Jewish or anti-Semitic measures would be modified. There have been promises that a Yiddish-language press (abolished in a Stalin anti-Jewish purge of 1949) would be re-established. Whether the elimination of Khrushchev from the scene would affect the situation was not immediately clear.

The general alienation of the younger generation from party goals and Soviet ideology confronts the Kremlin leadership with possibly its gravest internal crisis. If after more than four decades of education, propaganda and conditioning the young people seek their ideals, whether of dress or of morals, in the West rather than in the gospel of Marx and Lenin, the party faces the disintegration, sooner or later, of the philosophical basis of the regime.

Many of the thoughtful Soviet young people say they do not want to turn their back on the "ideals" of Communism. They want, instead, to see them realized. They say the "uncles" have lost all connection with ideals of any kind.

Whether the Soviet Union can effectively maintain leadership of a world Communist movement and carry the message of Communism to the rising peoples of Africa, Asia and Latin America while its own younger generation is moving so strongly away from submission to a dictated system of ethics, morals and artistic standards is an open question.

VIII

East Is East and West Is West

IMPROBABLE as it may seem, England's poet of Empire, Rudyard Kipling, has long been popular in the Soviet Union and of late Russians have taken to quoting to foreigners Kipling's lines (as they pronounce them):

> ". . . East is East, and Vest is Vest,
> And never the tvain shall meet . . ."

This, the Russians suggest, epitomizes the Soviet-Chinese situation.

When Premier Khrushchev was ousted, international speculation centered on the possibility that the Russians and the Chinese would patch up their quarrel and once more present a united front to the

world. Both sides promptly toned down the vituper-
ative propaganda in which they had been indulg-
ing. Premier Chou En-lai flew to Moscow to stand
on Lenin's tomb with the other chiefs of world
Communism on the Bolshevik holiday, November
7. There were several days of frantic conferences.
Then Chou flew back home. And soon thereafter
the Peking and Moscow propaganda guns resumed
fire.

It has been a constant source of puzzlement in
the West why the two Communist goliaths cannot
get along together. Signs of a rift were long evident, but so certain were most observers that self-
interest would keep the two powers working in
harness that the clues were discarded.

Indeed, it was not until I paid an unprecedented
visit to Outer Mongolia in 1959 and there saw
with my own eyes visible evidence of competition,
hostility and conflict that I was convinced that the
Soviet Union and China had parted company. In
Mongolia it was evident that the two nations were
behaving like typical imperialist rivals, each trying
to outmaneuver the other and win domination over
this underpopulated land of less than a million
people.

Earlier than this, in 1954, I had been amazed on
a lengthy trip along the Trans-Siberian Railroad as
far east as Khabarovsk to find that the great Soviet

garrisons which had long been maintained in the area as a defense against a thrust by Japan from Manchuria were being held at full strength, even though the only nearby power was China, the U.S.S.R.'s quondam friend and ally.

In trips to the same area in 1959 and again in 1961 I found that security precautions had been re-doubled. Plane flights across the Soviet frontier after dark were not permitted. Movement across the border was strictly controlled. Chinese traffic in and out of the Soviet Union had been reduced to a trickle, but each Chinese was subjected to the most careful scrutiny. His luggage and effects were ex-amined more thoroughly than my trunks ever had been at the height of Stalin's security phobia.

What is the source of the conflict between Peking and Moscow? All sorts of guesses have been haz-arded. The Russians and Chinese are not tradi-tional friends. Up to the end of the Czarist regime Imperial Russia gnawed away steadily at the disin-tegrating corpus of the once great Chinese Empire. The Communists were slow to give up their special advantages in north China. In fact Stalin insisted on maintaining the U.S.S.R.'s special position in Port Arthur, Darien, north China and Manchuria even after Mao Tse-tung came to power in Peking. Stalin insisted on joint stock companies for explora-tion and exploitation of China's resources, particularly in Sinkiang Province, where the Russians, both Czarist and Communist, had long been active.

Stalin was never friendly with Mao. At one time early in Mao's career, Stalin sought to oust him. He gave him little aid during the nineteen-thirties. During World War II Stalin maintained close relations with Chiang Kai-shek and after the war tried to get Mao to submit to Chiang's leadership. He admitted after Mao's victory that he had guessed wrong, that he had thought Chiang would win the postwar fight for power in China. There is even evidence that Stalin may have intrigued to undermine Mao after he came power, possibly by detaching Manchuria. Indeed, the Korean war may actually have been a by-product of Stalinist intrigues against Mao.

Despite all this, Stalin and Mao did sign in 1950 a treaty of friendship, mutual assistance and aid under which the Soviet Union was obligated to come to China's aid if China was attacked by Japan or any power allied with Japan (i.e., the United States).

Besides not being traditional friends, the U.S.S.R. and China offer conflicting interpretations of Communism to the world, especially in the field of foreign relations. Soviet policy has been based for some years on the doctrine of peaceful coexistence with the West, on the theory that great-power nuclear war can and must be prevented (because it would produce a world holocaust) and on the proposition that the process of transforming a capitalist world into a Communist world need not necessarily involve bloodshed and violent revolution. China has held the view that peaceful coexistence with capitalist countries is a contradiction in terms, that the nuclear danger is minimal because the "East Wind Prevails over the West Wind" (in other words, the Communist powers are stronger than the non-Communist powers) and that only by bloodshed and violence can true revolutions take place. The Russians say there is no alternative to negotiating with the West and particularly with the United States. The Chinese say that negotiations are hypocritical and can result only in surrender of Communist principles.

Fundamental as these differences are, there is good reason to believe that the key to the Moscow-Peking conflict is to be found neither in past relations between the Soviet and Chinese Communist parties nor in antipodal interpretations of Marxist doctrine.

As the dispute waxed, it acquired more and more of the overtones of great-power conflict. The border precautions which I had observed more than 10 years ago in Siberia took on meaning with repeated accounts in both the Chinese and the Soviet press of actual clashes along the frontier.

Chinese forces seized a group of islands in the Amur River, which forms the boundary between the two nations for a considerable distance north of Manchuria. The islands had long been occupied by the Russians. Up to 20,000 non-Chinese natives of Sinkiang Province fled across the frontier to the Soviet Union to take refuge with their Kirghis and Kazakh cousins, charging that the Chinese were persecuting them. The Chinese accused the Russians of fomenting trouble in Sinkiang. A pitched battle was fought at a rail transit point between Chinese train crews trying to bring propaganda leaflets into the U.S.S.R. and Soviet border troops determined to keep the leaflets out.

Incidents such as these were widely publicized internally by both countries. The Russians printed atrocity stories about the treatment that had been given by Chinese to the refugees from Sinkiang. The Russians also published accounts by Soviet engineers of the indignities they had suffered while working in China. Inside China hostility against Russians was fanned to such a point that Chinese attacked white Russians on the streets in cities like Mukden which had had small Russian minority populations for decades.

Propaganda of this type as well as the clashes which give rise to it is conventional between two countries seeking to stir their citizens to hatred of each other. It is the normal prelude to full-scale crisis or hostilities.

What brought relations between the U.S.S.R. and China to this point?

The answer probably is contained in two revealing statements made in late summer and early autumn of 1964, the first by Mao Tse-tung and the second by Khrushchev. Both statements were made to Japanese delegations which chanced to be visiting, respectively, Peking and Moscow.

Placed in juxtaposition, the two statements made it clear that in the autumn of 1954, when Khrushchev and his then traveling companion Marshal Bulganin visited Peking for the first time, they were confronted by a demand to discuss territorial issues. Khrushchev revealed that he had summarily refused to negotiate on any such question.

What were the territories?

They constituted most of eastern Siberia, the lands north of the Amur River (the so-called Maritime Provinces), Outer Mongolia and about half of Soviet Central Asia.

The territories contain Soviet populations of more than 25 million.

The Chinese contend that all of the regions once were under the sway of the Chinese Empire. They claim that Russia detached the areas from China through a series of unequal treaties, imposed on the weakened empire by physical force during the 19th century. The Chinese maintain that none of these treaties was ever accepted as binding by Peking.

Outer Mongolia, of course, is a quasi-independent country, officially called since 1924 the Mongolian People's Republic. It has been under Russia's nominal protection most of the time since just before World War I. However, the Chinese claimed that Stalin compelled Chiang Kai-shek to relinquish China's claims to sovereignty as part of the diplomatic maneuvering that accompanied the Soviet Union's entry into the war against Japan.

The Chinese do not dispute Khrushchev's contention that the territorial question was raised. In fact, Chinese maps used in Chinese schools since 1949 have depicted all of these regions as detached from China by unjust and unequal treaty. Peking lists nine unequal treaties imposed upon China by the Great European Powers. The first three of these were imposed by Russia.

Why should China jeopardize its relations with the U.S.S.R. over these obscure territorial claims? Are they to be compared with the ill consequences that followed the Soviet Union's withdrawal of material, technical and military support in the years beginning in 1959?

The answer seems clearly embedded in China's

population problem, which may well be the world's single most important political fact. China now has a population of close to 750 million. This population increases at a rate of more than 20 million a year. Before 1975 China's people will number more than one billion. The pressures generated are enormous. China already is severely pressed to find food for its multitudes. Each year makes the problem more critical. One solution—possibly the only solution—is to find land where the surplus population can be settled and where new sources of food can be obtained.

The largely vacant Soviet lands, the easily arable grassland plateaus of Mongolia, offer a tempting prospect. Tens of millions of Chinese could be resettled. The population pressure could be eased indefinitely.

If this is the real source of the Chinese-Soviet dispute, it will not yield to easy solution.

The course of the quarrel supports this analysis. There have been repeated efforts at compromise and mediation. Each time the trouble has merely grown worse. There are no signs that the conferences during Chou En-lai's visit to Moscow in November, 1964, followed a different pattern.

The best opinion in Moscow holds that Khrushchev's successors merely wanted to make plain to the rest of the Communist world that the onus for the Chinese-Soviet split did not rest with them alone, and that, regardless of the personal venom poured into the quarrel by Khrushchev, they were willing to make any reasonable gesture to ease the tensions. In other words, Moscow sought to strengthen its position within the world Communist movement, not to appease Peking.

There is, however, good reason to believe that Krushchev's cavalier handling of the quarrel played a part in his downfall. He managed matters so that Moscow not only came to the breaking point with Peking but also lost major support within the Communist world. No longer does Moscow hold the leadership of the Communist camp as it did under Stalin. Rebellion is common among Western Communist parties. Disarray is the rule in Eastern Europe. In Asia many Communist parties have openly gone over to Peking.

Khrushchev's successors still show no signs of any desire to appease Peking. Their position vis-à-vis the Chinese is nationalistic, almost chauvinistic. The anti-Chinese posture is popular with the Soviet citizenry. Since the time of the Mongols the Russians have had little faith, trust or friendship for peoples from the east. They make few distinctions between the Mongols of Genghis Khan and the Chinese of Mao Tse-tung.

The Kremlin leaders' quarrel with Khrushchev

was not over the question of a break with Peking. It was over the weakening of the Soviet position within the Communist world generally. This was a point of special tenderness with the military high command. The Soviet marshals took the line that their defense commitments had been doubled at a single stroke. They were compelled to take steps against possible hostilities with China along a front of thousands of miles in distant Siberia at the same time their defensive bastions in Eastern Europe were being weakened by the onset of Communist diversity as a by-product of the quarrel with Peking.

The deep involvement of Moscow and Peking in a dispute which manifests itself on so many levels —ideological, geographical, ethnic, historical, territorial, philosophical, economic, diplomatic—can be expected to color almost every move the Soviet Union undertakes both internationally and domestically for the foreseeable future. Regardless of efforts to ameliorate Soviet-Chinese differences, they almost certainly will slowly but steadily worsen. The ultimate outcome may well be military.

IX

The Many Gospels of Communism

NOT MANY MONTHS after Nikita Khrushchev delivered his anti-Stalin speech in February, 1956, the late Palmiro Togliatti, leader of the Italian Communist party, gave a talk which is not nearly so well known. The subject of his remarks was what he called "polycentrism."

The essence of Togliatti's theme was that Communism no longer had a single source, a Mecca to which all turned for guidance. Each national Communist movement now was developing its own form and content, its individual approach to the problems of a particular country. No longer did each movement wait for orders from Moscow or consult with the Kremlin on each change in policy.

Moscow denounced Togliatti's views—at the time. But they proved to contain a far-sighted vision of precisely what has happened within the Communist world.

Actually the tendency toward a splintering of Communism began before Stalin's death, when Yugoslavia's Marshal Tito broke with Moscow and set out to show that national Communism was possible even in a Balkan country deficient in national resources. Since 1948 the Yugoslavs have made a fetish of developing their own solutions to Communist problems, including healthy admixtures of ordinary capitalist profit-making motivations and liberal use of Western aid and advice in resolving difficult economic and social questions.

Tito's independent Communism still sets the pattern of the disparate winds blowing through the Communist world. It is a Communism based on maintaining relations on both sides of the fence, East and West. It stresses contacts and connections with the emerging African and Asian nations and seeks to move toward a "Third Force" which would play an independent role in world politics, committed neither to Moscow nor Washington nor Peking.

The extension of the conflict between the Soviet Union and China has given enormous momentum to polycentrism within the Communist world. The second Communist state to break out of the pattern of strict subservience to Moscow was Albania, the tiny Adriatic neighbor of Yugoslavia. The Albanians, largely for nationalistic reasons (closely connected with a blood feud against the Yugoslavs), broke with Moscow and set up an independent connection with Peking. Just as Yugoslavia represents the most liberal or Westernized type of Communist state, so Albania is the most Stalinist and repressive of Communist states.

The defection of these two segments of what once constituted Stalin's Balkan Empire has been followed by spreading disarray in Eastern Europe. Rumania has taken up a kind of halfway house between Moscow and Peking, having revolted against an effort by the Soviet Union to impose upon her a pattern of agrarian concentration which conflicted with her aspirations to develop as a more highly industrialized state.

As an outgrowth of this revolt the Rumanians have entered into extensive trade and cultural relations with the West, particularly the United States. And the late Gheorghe Gheorghiu-Dej, the wily Rumanian leader, opened up a flirtation with Marshal Tito looking toward the establishment of a more independent Balkan Communist bloc which would align itself fundamentally with Gamal Abdel Nasser's Egypt, with India and with some of the new

African powers.

Both Poland and Hungary won for themselves a substantial measure of national independence within the Communist bloc as a result of their uprisings in 1956. The Polish gains were won outright by Wladyslaw Gomulka, Poland's Communist leader, in his famous confrontation with Khrushchev at a moment when Soviet tanks were advancing on Warsaw. Poland's Communism has contained a far more liberal mixture of artistic and creative freedom than exists in Moscow even today. It has been based on the free-enterprise system for the peasant and has permitted a substantial degree of private endeavor in small-scale service trade. Polish diplomatic policy has demonstrated a degree of inventiveness, particularly in connection with the so-called Rapacki plan for a neutralized nuclear-free zone in Central and Eastern Europe. Hungary's rebels were crushed by Khrushchev's tanks in 1956 and the Janos Kadar regime was imposed on the sullen Hungarians. However, with the passage of years the Kadar Government has taken its place as the most liberal in Eastern Europe, exceeding the permissiveness of Poland. It, too, is experimenting with its own kind of Communism.

Of the Eastern European countries those still attached fairly strongly to the U.S.S.R. are East Ger-

many (in the Moscow camp by necessity but ideo-
logically nearer to Peking), Bulgaria, which has
strong cultural and ethnic connections with Russia,
and Czechoslovakia, which shows little inclination
to strike out on an independent course.

The free-wheeling in Eastern Europe has made
the area no longer a secure bastion for Soviet defense. The ability of regimes to play Moscow
against Peking and vice versa has given all of them
greater independence. And an increasingly flexible
U.S. policy has stimulated the Rumanians, Poles
and Hungarians to explore actively the potentials of
increased polycentrism.

But the effects of the polycentric tendency have
by no means been confined to Eastern Europe. Togliatti died while on vacation in the Soviet Union in
the summer of 1964, but not before delivering another prophetic declaration, this one a warning to
Moscow that its policies in the dispute with Peking
were leading toward the total disintegration of the
world Communist movement—words likely to
prove as far-reaching as those he had earlier ut-
tered about polycentrism.

Togliatti's own Italian Communist Party, the
largest in Europe, was already well advanced on
the route to independent Communism. It took the
liberty of sharply rebuking Moscow for its stric-
tures against writers and poets in 1963. It criticized

the manner in which the Moscow party Presidium announced the removal of Khrushchev, and it went out of its way to praise Khrushchev's positive services to the party. It encouraged a notably tolerant attitude toward religion and particularly the Catholic Church and—breaking with Moscow—said that a man's religious faith was his own business. While rebuking Khrushchev's tactics against the Chinese, the Italians took the most anti-Chinese of positions.

Much the same line emerged in Europe's second strongest Communist party—that of France. It, too, began to mold its tactics and philosophies to a French rather than Russian pattern. All over the Western world the smaller Communist parties started to show their independence by questioning Moscow policies. They criticized Moscow for intolerance of religion. They denounced Moscow for anti-Semitism. They demanded greater frankness in facing the issues of Stalinism and less hypocrisy in discussing Khrushchev.

The criticism of Moscow from what might be termed a "liberal" Communist position became almost a hallmark of the Western parties. But in Asia and the East just the reverse was true. Here the influence of geography, the propinquity of China and, no doubt, the comparative backwardness of the social systems involved led Communist parties to criticize Moscow from a Stalinist position and to move steadily into acceptance of leadership from Peking, not the Kremlin.

Thus, the North Korean party, which had been established by the Russians and which had loyally followed every turn in Moscow policy, moved first into a position of neutrality and then openly sided with Peking. The big Indonesian Communist party, the largest in Asia (outside of China), went over to the Peking side despite strenuous efforts by Khrushchev and his chief ideological lieutenant, Mikhail A. Suslov. The Japanese Communist party joined the Chinese camp. So did the parties in Burma and Ceylon. The party in India split and, revealing the nationalistic bias of Communists, the dominant segment adhered to Moscow and firmly opposed Peking.

In Mongolia, caught between the giant mill-stones of the Soviet Union and China, there arose three well-defined factions: (1) the ruling group, trained in Moscow and staunch allies of the Kremlin; (2) a group of strong nationalists hoping to employ the Moscow-Peking split to win more national independence for Mongolia and possibly even to establish a Greater Mongolia incorporating minorities in the Soviet Union and China; and (3) a pro-Chinese faction. Intrigue and the maneuvering of the U.S.S.R. and China brought about frequent shifts in the Mongol power structure.

Throughout Asia there was a tendency to choose sides between the contending Communist giants. In general the more militant and revolutionary movements sided with Peking, the more nationalistic with Moscow. The Soviet Union pursued in Asia a policy that differed sharply from China's. The Russians sought to woo nationalist regimes and concentrated especially on welding a firm friendship with India, obviously as a bulwark against the expansion of Chinese influence. Indeed, one of the major causes of increasing friction between Moscow and Peking was the Kremlin's support of India in the Chinese-Indian border quarrel. The Russians continued to give India strong economic support even while withdrawing such aid from China. And when China attacked India's northern frontier, Moscow reaffirmed its determination to supply India with warplanes and other arms.

The Soviet policy in Asia was based, for the most part, upon links to governments rather than to revolutionary movements. The Communist parties under Moscow influence were largely supporters of national liberation governments—regimes which succeeded colonial rulers. Those under Peking influence often were opposed to the national governments and sought to undermine them by revolutionary tactics.

The contrast took on sharp overtones in Southeast Asia. There the North Vietnamese leader Ho Chi Minh was Moscow-trained. He sought for a long time to maintain his lines to Moscow although geography forced him to keep relations with Peking cordial. Gradually, however, Ho found himself being pulled into the Chinese sphere. At the same time the Russians, who had sought to ease Southeast Asian tensions in order to minimize Chinese possibilities for fishing in troubled waters, found themselves propelled into a more and more militant attitude to keep the Chinese from taking over North Vietnam completely.

The Russians felt highly sensitive to Chinese contentions that they lacked revolutionary ardor. Consequently, as the Vietnam fighting increased in severity, Moscow felt compelled to reaffirm repeatedly its utmost determination to support North Vietnam in every way against any direct move by the United States.

The Soviet-Chinese competition in Vietnam, which tended to increase the tempo of fighting, provided an example in microcosm of one of the most serious side-effects of the conflict between the two goliaths of Communism.

In Asia and Africa and to an increasing extent in Latin America, Moscow and Peking found themselves engaged in a desperate battle for control of the revolutionary elements in the population. In many places this meant the Communist movement. In others it meant nationalist elements.

Increasingly, in country after country there was set up an affiliate of Moscow and an affiliate of Peking. The Communist movement became bifurcated. Moscow sought to use its superior economic power and its international prestige to win diplomatic and trade alliances with new national regimes. But where actual hostilities or revolutions were involved—as in Vietnam and the Congo—the intervention of both Moscow and Peking rapidly assumed a more openly military character.

The Soviet Union utilized the prestige of its new-found space leadership and its massive nuclear and rocket power to the ultimate in the competition with China. It placed the vast experience of its engineers, won in the continental effort to transform Russia into a modern state, at the disposal of emerging nations like Egypt and India. In this game Peking lacked the capital, the raw materials and the technical know-how to match Moscow.

But China had another weapon: race. First quietly and gradually more openly the Chinese preached to the emerging nations that color should form a basis for solidarity, that the brown, black and yellow races of the world had to unite against the white, against the Europeans. The Russians in

Africa suddenly found themselves bracketed with the British, French and Belgian colonialists. In Asia the Soviet Union found itself lumped with England, France and Germany as the imperial powers which had despoiled that continent during the 19th century when both India and China were too weak to resist.

The Chinese argument was bulwarked with the valid and realistic contention that the U.S.S.R. was an advanced Western nation, that it had little real interest in helping the backward countries of the world move forward, that it was primarily concerned with raising Soviet standards of living (Khrushchev was cited on this point), that it would not even help China, its fellow Communist nation, in the long hard pull to industrialization.

The Cuban crisis of the autumn of 1962 became a central theme in Chinese propaganda. Peking declared that Moscow had no real interest in building up the Castro regime in Cuba or in spreading the Castro revolution to others parts of Latin America. By removing Soviet missiles from Cuba, said Peking, Khrushchev had quailed before American nuclear power, had been unwilling to risk a fight for the sake of his Cuban revolutionary comrades. If Khrushchev was not willing to fight for Castro, how unlikely it was that he would really risk anything for any genuine revolutionary cause anywhere—so ran the Chinese argument.

Moscow felt vulnerable to this line of attack. It was notable after Cuba that the Russians went to great pains to insist on their true revolutionary zeal. They believed they had no alternative. If the emerging revolutionaries around the world accepted the Chinese statements as true, then Moscow would quickly lose leadership of the Communist movement in many areas to the Chinese.

The truth of the matter was that the Soviet Union had become a status quo country. The Bolshevik Revolution was long in the past. The revolutionaries were old. A generation was in power in Moscow which had only childhood memories of the events of 1917. They took the position that the U.S.S.R. had had to make its way on its own. It was up to the new generation of revolutionaries, those of China, to fight their way forward as Lenin and his associates had done in the grim days of the early Bolshevik era.

The Russians were not by nature particularly sympathetic to the aspirations of either the Chinese or the Africans. They had deep fears and suspicions of the Chinese, fears ingrained in their national heritage.

Nor did they feel on close acquaintance any great empathy for the Africans. The Russians have long prided themselves on an absence of race feelings, particularly with regard to Negroes. Negroes have always been extremely rare in Russia. Not more than a few hundred have ever lived there. These few, many of them originally from the United States, have been almost idolized. Russian sympathies for Negroes had long been warm, fed by countless stories of racial hatred and incidents in the United States.

Then came Russia's first exposure to large numbers of Negroes—African students coming to Moscow to study in the special university named for the martyred Patrice Lumumba, the Congo's murdered leftist Premier. Almost overnight racial feelings appeared among ordinary Russians. Students at the university harassed Russian girls who went on dates with the Africans. Africans reported warnings from Russian students not to go out with Russian classmates. To minimize contacts and thus reduce incidents between Russian and African students, special dormitories and recreational facilities were set up.

Then an even uglier event occurred. An African student died during the frigid winter of 1963—the cause is still a matter of dispute. The Russians contend he was drunk, fell off a suburban train and died of exposure. The Africans say he was going steady with a Russian girl, was set upon and beaten to death.

Whatever the facts, the African's death produced a spectacle Russians had not seen since the revolution—a spontaneous demonstration in Red Square. It was conducted by African students carrying banners denouncing the Russians and demanding justice.

But the incident did not inspire Russians with sympathy for the cause of their black brothers. Instead it evoked hatred and racist sentiments. Ordinary Russians called the students "black apes." They demanded to know why good Russian money was being spent on "such savages."

The Soviet Government did its utmost to hush up the affair and minimize its harsh propaganda aspects. But the plain truth of Russian chauvinism and nationalism could not be concealed.

It came to the fore again late in 1964 when African students, on instructions of Communist party propagandists, demonstrated in front of the American, British and Belgian Embassies in Moscow to protest the airlift that rescued white hostages of the Congolese rebels. Russians watching the African students hurl stones and inkpots at the embassies spat and muttered once again about "monkeys" and "illiterate heathens."

In the face of national sentiments so strongly and widely held, the Soviet Union's task of holding its own against Chinese competition in Asia and

Africa seemed more and more difficult.

It was against this background that an event occurred in October, 1964, which many Asians believe has tipped the balance irretrievably in China's favor. This was the successful test by the Chinese of a nuclear device. To Asians this was possibly the greatest event of the century. It was a demonstration that Asia had caught up with the West. As one Western-oriented Indian put it: "The first great event for Asia occurred in 1905. It was the sinking of the Russian fleet at Tsushima by the Japanese. For the first time we Asians saw a rift of hope in the clouds. Now China has cleared the skies. Asia speaks with a voice that at last equals that of Europe and America."

In the West the Chinese nuclear test was minimized. It was noted that what had been tested was merely a device, that to produce a bomb requires time, to produce an armory of bombs requires years, to produce advanced delivery techniques is far beyond China's current capabilities.

But in Asia—and in Africa—the Chinese test took on a different coloration. It was a portent of a day when Asian and African heads can be held as high as any in the world.

China's nuclear power may well be the ace which gives Peking world leadership of the dispossessed and poverty-stricken nations, and almost certainly it gives Peking an ace in the competition with Moscow for leadership of the revolutionary factions in these nations.

X

Whither Russia?

THE QUESTION of Russia's future has preoccupied Russians—and the world—for generations. For better than a century Russian poets and philosophers have been asking it and often adding: What shall we do? What is to be done?

Far more than most countries, Russia has been troubled about the future. She has been for as long as the world can remember a nation in motion, a nation moody and unfulfilled, a nation with a deep sense of mission (this was as well defined under the Czars as it was to be under the Communists), a nation which—because of her size, her problems, her attitude toward other peoples and her own— has caused statesmen and diplomats sleepless nights and frequent conferences.

In the mirror that Russian writers have held up to Russia they have seen their nation whirling through space and time like a mighty troika, coming from nowhere and bound for God knows where; they have envisaged the Russian people as a mighty force arising from the elemental steppes of Asia and pouring out over the settled plains of Europe; they have seen Russia as a giant, powerful but stumbling, filled with promise, potent with dread.

These visions and preoccupations tell us an important fact: The Russian problem is not a new one; it has been with us for a long time. It will probably remain for a long time.

What nature is it likely to assume in the new era about to unfold?

For the first decade after World War II relations between the Soviet Union and the West were dominated almost exclusively by preoccupation with the threat of Soviet expansionism.

The threat arose almost before the war was over. The Iranian crisis, the Greek civil strife, the danger to Turkey came before the sound of bombing in Western Europe had completely died away.

The West began frantically to erect barriers to the Communist challenge. The Marshall Plan created an economic foundation for defense efforts.

Then came the military pacts that culminated in the North Atlantic Treaty Organization in which the United States and Western Europe made common cause against the Soviet threat.

NATO proved its usefulness in the Berlin blockade of 1948. It held firm against repeated subsequent tests by the Soviet Union. Gradually the United States set up a worldwide system of alliances designed to contain the Communist thrust—alliances such as the Central Treaty Organization and the Southeast Asia Treaty Organization.

With the countering of the Communists in Korea the picture began to change. The period of intensive military challenge began to fade into an enduring era of diplomatic confrontation erected basically upon the balance of nuclear and missile power possessed by the United States and the Soviet Union.

It is against this military and diplomatic background that the world takes up the task of attempting to envision what future form the Communist challenge may assume.

A strong school of thought holds the view that in the redistribution of world power taking place as a result of the rapid rise of China and of new nations in Africa and Asia the Soviet Union will be propelled toward the West. Indeed, there are already visible indications that, regardless of efforts to maintain status as the chief source of revolutionary spirit in the world, the U.S.S.R. has already moved a substantial distance into the European community. There has been a similar movement of most of the Eastern European states closely associated with Moscow.

This development is explained by some in historical terms. For instance, George F. Kennan, the distinguished diplomat and student of Russian affairs, believes that for nearly 100 years leading up to 1917 Russia was preparing for a liberal, democratic revolution which would link her destiny firmly with that of the liberal, democratic states of what we know now as the Atlantic community—Western Europe and the Western Hemisphere.

It was, in Mr. Kennan's opinion, a bitter and almost a chance stroke of fate that the Russian revolution was captured by Lenin and his radical Bolsheviks, who thus tore Russia from the tracks on which it was moving and diverted it into a radical dictatorial state.

His analysis suggests that with the death of Stalin, the rise of more liberal tendencies within the Soviet state and the development of polycentrism in the Communist world, Russia is moving back toward the path she was destined to follow.

This movement of the U.S.S.R. toward the West has been accelerated by the dynamics of its quarrel with China—a quarrel which, as we have seen, is likely to intensify, affecting not only relations between the two superstates but their relations to other countries, particularly those of Asia and Africa.

Many Russians have frankly spoken for several years of their fears that the Chinese-Soviet conflict may, in the end, result in war. Many Russians have openly told foreigners of their fear that a nuclear-armed China would prove an even more aggressive and difficult world power than it has been thus far. The Russians have hinted to Americans that it would be wise for the United States and the Soviet Union to act to halt the spread of nuclear weapons before China becomes fully armed. Once China is so armed, in their opinion, it would be too late or too difficult.

The conduct of China since it carried out its first nuclear test has tended to reinforce strongly these Russian suggestions. China has become more, not less, belligerent. It has become more, not less, intransigent toward the United States. It has engaged in assaults on the United Nations which strongly suggest that if offered membership in that body Peking would promptly reject it.

The Soviet conflict with China has brought to the Russians an increasing consciousness of their European heritage. They now speak of themselves as Europeans, not Asiatics (as Stalin once did to the Japanese Foreign Minister). They challenge the contention of Alexander Blok's famous poem "The Scythians" that "We, too, are Asiatics." With the increased ease of travel Russians are renewing their cultural bonds with Europe.

These tendencies hold deep significance for the future of Soviet-American relations. If China is emerging as a great power hostile to both the U.S.S.R. and the United States, Moscow and Washington for the first time since World War II will begin to have a common security interest.

The international scene confronts the Kremlin with an extraordinarily difficult task. Since the Soviet Union is a Communist state with links to Communist movements everywhere, Moscow is determined to maintain these connections wherever it can. The Russians are fighting the Chinese on literally 100 fronts to control the international Communist movement and, more than that, to maintain leadership so far as possible of the strongly nationalistic nations which have appeared in former colonial areas.

Over the long run, it would seem, the Russians will not be able to have the world both ways. That is, the more the U.S.S.R. emphasizes its role as a European power, the less effective will be the Soviet campaign to maintain control of African and Asian

Communism and the more effectively will Peking challenge Moscow for leadership of the nationalist movements.

However, if China's aggressive policy leads her into actual war against neighboring countries in Asia—should, for example, hostilities again break out on the Indian frontier, should China in a lightning stroke take over Burma, should the Chinese succeed in fomenting a successful pro-Chinese coup in Mongolia—the fears of new nations that they might be swallowed by their erstwhile Chinese friends are likely to be stimulated.

Moscow's ability to cater to backward nations with large-scale aid programs is considerable. But this, too, is hindered by the rising and seemingly irresistible demands within the Soviet populace for a higher standard of living. Since the U.S.S.R. already suffers from chronic difficulty in getting its system to function well enough to provide for all its needs, the increasing domestic pressures place an effective limit on the flexibility of Soviet foreign-aid policy.

The combination of these factors may well impose substantial ceilings on Soviet challenges to the United States in the next decade.

However, the twists and turns which may be taken by two international Communist movements, one allied with Moscow and one with Peking, in manipulating and stimulating anti-Western campaigns around the world are certain to keep U.S. policymakers preoccupied.

One area in which a test of rival Communist influence is likely is Cuba. Moscow has given Castro the economic support his regime has needed for survival. But Peking is much closer to the Cuban revolution in terms of ideology. The Chinese have worked steadily since the 1962 Cuban crisis to displace the Russians in Havana. In January, 1965, China signed a special five-year economic pact with Cuba. Peking is still not able to replace Moscow as a reliable economic prop. But the time may not be far distant when China, regardless of the sacrifice at home, might find it politically desirable to offer Castro all-out economic aid in return for his adherence to a Chinese Communist International. At the least the Chinese have been able to increase Castro's bargaining power with Moscow by enabling him to employ the threat of closer ties with Peking as a lever for extracting more aid from the Russians.

Another test of Chinese-Soviet strength is in the making in Africa. Both the Soviet Union and China have supported the Congolese rebels.

It is not accidental that the areas in which the Chinese-Soviet rivalry has emerged with intensity are precisely those where U.S. security concerns are high—Cuba, the Congo, Vietnam. It is in the

world's trouble spots that Communist involvement is
to be expected. Under present-day conditions the
crises are more and more likely to be three-way—a
confrontation between the United States and the
Communist challenge complicated by a conflict between the Communist challengers themselves.

Will this dual Communist threat be minimized
by an easing of Soviet-American tensions?

This is a field already undergoing intensive exploration. The United States has made a series of
moves aimed at establishing whether the U.S.S.R.
might be interested in stabilization of relations
with the West. President Johnson in his January,
1965, State of the Union Message proposed active
steps in this direction, including exchanges of visits at high levels as a way to increase mutual knowledge and confidence.

Formidable obstacles remain, however, to the
achievement of broad rapprochement. It was evident during the Khrushchev regime that whenever
an approach was made toward basic settlements it
encountered almost inevitable barriers. Indeed, not
infrequently tensions rose as a result of efforts to
approach such impacted questions as Berlin or the
Communist regimes in Eastern Europe.

Any effort by Washington to resolve outstanding quarrels with Moscow causes concern to rise in
West Germany. The West Germans view such en-

deavors as likely to undermine their preferred position as the chief bulwark of U.S. defense arrangements in Europe.

At the same time the lack of any settlement of the issue of divided Germany tends constantly to feed basic insecurity in Eastern Europe, where the Poles and Czechs still worry that a resurgent Germany might again plunge Europe into war. The Russians both play on these fears and share them.

Despite the intractability of the German question, marked progress toward an identity of views on nuclear questions has been made by Moscow and Washington, and further progress is generally held a prerequisite to any broader stabilization of confidence.

Some diplomats contend that the principal obstacle in the nuclear field now lies in Moscow. The Russians, preoccupied with their quarrel and competition with China, hesitate to take any step that might be used against them by Peking. The Chinese have fashioned effective propaganda out of their contention that the Russians have been made dupes in their negotiations with Washington and that the advantage in the limited nuclear test ban treaty concluded in 1963 went to the West.

On the Soviet side there is a further inhibiting factor. Political stability in the U.S.S.R. after a change in leadership requires a considerable period

for attainment. It took roughly three years a͟f͟t͟e͟r͟ t͟h͟e͟
death of Stalin before Khrushchev emerge͟d͟ a͟s͟ a͟
strong chief, running affairs on his own. T͟h͟e͟ i͟n͟
terim had been filled with short-lived an͟d͟ o͟f͟t͟e͟n͟
contradictory policies, frequent periods in which
action was suspended because of an interna͟l͟ (͟a͟n͟d͟
frequently not well understood) Kremlin p͟o͟w͟e͟r͟
crisis and efforts by Moscow factions to use o͟n͟e͟ p͟o͟l͟
icy or another to their advantage.

A similar period of instability was touch͟e͟d͟ o͟f͟f͟
by the displacement of Khrushchev. While th͟e͟ P͟r͟e͟
sidium of the party was virtually unanimous i͟n͟ p͟u͟t͟t͟
ing Khrushchev out, the coalition was by no m͟e͟a͟n͟s͟
agreed on many other issues. Nor was it ap͟p͟a͟r͟e͟n͟t͟
to the Presidium or the Central Committee o͟r͟ t͟h͟e͟
party what degree of support Brezhnev or K͟o͟s͟y͟g͟i͟n͟
would be able to muster over the long run.

In such a period Soviet action in the interna͟t͟i͟o͟n͟a͟l͟
field tends to be restricted in much the sam͟e͟ w͟a͟y͟
American action is during a Presidential cam͟p͟a͟i͟g͟n͟
year or a time when there is a very close di͟v͟i͟s͟i͟o͟n͟
of votes in Congress. There is a tendency to͟ c͟o͟n͟
tinue with existing policy and to be wary of͟ n͟e͟w͟
commitments because of the implications the͟y͟ m͟a͟y͟
bear on the balance of power in the Kremlin.

Nevertheless, the struggle-for-power perio͟d͟ i͟n͟
Moscow is a time of international stress becau͟s͟e͟ i͟t͟

the possibility of sudden and unexpected moves on the foreign scene designed to advance the personal fortunes of one of the contenders for the top spot.

There is always a risk in this situation that a man may push himself to the top with a program which has the open backing of forces favorable to a reinstitution of Stalinist methods at home and rapprochement with China in the international sphere. Such a development would bring to the world dangers even more grave than those which arise from competition between the two Communist giants.

However, the possibility of a fundamental switch in Soviet foreign policy appears to be limited by factors of geography, ethnic bias, cultural and industrial development and popular orientation. With few exceptions, the major social forces in the Soviet Union clearly face West, not East. This acts as an inhibiting influence upon the rise of a leader who would turn in the other direction.

The last 100 years of Czarist Russia were given over in large measure to a struggle between contending groups—those who felt Russia's future was bound up irretrievably with Europe and those who felt that she had some mystic mission of her own, isolated from Europe and close to Asia. As long ago as the beginning of the 18th century Peter the Great built Russia a new capital, St. Petersburg, on the Gulf of Finland to give the country a "window on the West."

Peter felt that only by such drastic means could he shove his backward country into the West and into the modern world which, even then, advanced technology was creating. Two hundred years have passed. The Czars have fallen. Even the Communist regime has grown middle-aged. The struggle for Russia's soul has not yet been finally won, but a new generation of young Russians is rising which seeks its spiritual sustenance in the West and not in the harsh, fanatic atmosphere of Mao's Peking.

No one can be certain where a nation which spans two continents, whose history begins in the faint traces of early human civilization, a nation now struggling to find a new and valid philosophy of existence, will be propelled by the transcendental forces of the nuclear age. But by those qualities which can be objectively measured, the chances seem better that she will stand with those countries which seek a measure of order and security in the world than with those which put their hopes in elemental change and cosmic chaos.

INDEX

Adzhubei, Aleksei I., 43
Africa, 12, 48, 80, 94, 107, 109, 114, 117-18, 120, 127
Akhmadullina, Bella, 87
Aksyonov, Vasily, 88
Albania, 60, 108
American Relief Administration, 61
Amur River, 100, 101
Anderson, Sherwood, 88
Armenia (Union Republic), 28
Asia: opposes Communism, 21; Southeast, 114; *references to*, 12, 48, 80, 94, 107, 112ff, 120
Australia, 60
Azerbaijan (Union Republic), 28

"Babi Yar" (poem), 86, 92
Bakst, Lev N., 89
Balkan Communist bloc, 108
Beria, Lavrenti P., 32, 36
Blok, Alexander, 127

Bolsheviks, 14, 16, 18, 20, 64, 117, 125
Bolshoi Ballet, 41
Brezhnev, Leonid I., 12, 35, 46, 132
Budapest revolt of 1956, 42
Bulganin, Nikolai A., 32, 33, 34, 37, 101
Bulgaria, 58-59
Burma, 128
Burmese Communist party, 112
Byelorussia (Union Republic), 28-29

Castro, Fidel, 47, 116, 129
Central Committee. *See under* Communist party
Central Intelligence Agency, United States, 38
Central Treaty Organization, 124
Ceylonese Communist party, 112
Chagall, Marc, 89
Chaika (Russian automobile), 77

Cheever, John, 90

Chekhov, Anton P., 88, 89

Chiang Kai-shek, 21, 98, 102

China. *See* Communist China

Chinese Communist International, 129

Chou En-lai, 96, 103

Churchill, Winston, 29, 53

Communism: and centralized dictation, 13; future of, 18; and "The New Class," 45; *references to,* 4, 20, 24, 41ff, 50ff, 66, 72, 79, 80, 92, 94, 106-21, 122. *See also* Communist China; Communist party; Russia, future of

Communist China: eagerness to industrialize, 80; establishment of communes, 80; and Moscow-Peking split, 80, 95-105, 107ff, 125ff; and nuclear test, 120, 126; population of, 103; rapid rise of, 124; *references to,* 12, 21, 47-48, 57ff

Communist International, 21

Communist Manifesto, 4

Communist party: Burmese, 112; Central Committee, 30, 33, 44, 132; Ceylonese, 112; dictatorship by, 27; French, 111; Indian, 112; Indonesian, 112; Italian, 106; Japanese, 112; North Korean, 112; number of members, 30; Presidium, 23, 30, 33ff, 111, 132; *references to,* 12, 16, 26, 29-30, 36, 50ff, 82, 91, 93; Russian aloofness to, 44; Western, 104; Yugoslav, 44, 45. *See also* Communism; Communist China

Congo, 115, 118, 129

Constituent Republics. *See* Union Republics

Constitution of the Soviet Union, 27, 30

Cuba, 34, 57, 116, 129

Czars, Russia under: and anti-Semitism, 92; and fall of imperialism, 17; planning commission of 1915, 21; *references to,* 10, 15, 16, 23, 27, 29, 63, 65, 97, 122, 134

Czechoslovakia, 110

Djilas, Milovan, 44-45
Don River, 15
Dulles, Allen W., 38-39

East Germany, 109-10
Egypt, 108, 115
Ehrenburg, Ilya, 89
Eisenhower, Dwight D.,
    70-71
England, 18, 20, 116
Estonia (Union Republic),
    28, 29

Fathers and Sons (novel),
    82
Faulkner, William, 90
Fokine, Michel, 89
France, 18, 20, 115
French Communist party,
    111

Genghis Khan, 7, 104
Georgia (Union Republic),
    28, 52
Germany, 18-19, 21, 115;
    East, 109-10; West,
    130-31
Gheorghiu-Dej, Gheorghe,
    108
Gogol, Nikolai V., 89
Gomulka, Wladyslaw, 109
Gorky, Maxim, 89

Hemingway, Ernest, 88, 90
Ho Chi Minh, 114
Hoover, Herbert, 61
Hungary, 58; enforces col-
    lectivism, 59; opposes
    Communism, 21; poly-
    centric tendencies in,
    110; uprisings of 1956,
    109

India, 108, 113, 115, 128
Indian Communist party,
    112
Indonesian Communist
    party, 112
International Revolution, 4
Iron Curtain, 23
Italian Communist party,
    106
Ivan the Terrible, 6-7, 22-
    23
Izvestia (newspaper), 43

Japan, 20, 63, 96, 98, 102,
    120, 127
Japanese Communist party,
    112
Jewish religion in Russia,
    92. *See also* Russia,
    anti-Semitism in
Johnson, Lyndon B., 130

Kadar, Janos, 59, 109

Kamenev, Lev Borisovich, 35

Kandinsky, Vasily, 89

Kazakhstan (Union Republic), 10, 28, 58

Kazakov, Yuri, 88

Kennan, George F., 125

Kennedy, John F., 34

Kerensky, Aleksander, 17

Khrushchev, Nikita S.: and aid to Cuba, 47; becomes Soviet Premier, 10, 32; confronted by Gomulka, 109; criticized, 23; and Cuban debacle of 1962, 34, 116; denies anti-Semitic sentiments, 92; denounces Stalin, 26, 39, 42, 106; deposed, 12, 23, 26-27, 35, 37, 47, 95, 111; divides Russia into economic regions, 77; and efforts to decentralize industrial control, 77; and efforts to improve Russia, 10-11, 23, 116; enemies' plots to depose, 32-33; plans for Communism, 18, 48; *references to*, 5, 32ff, 43, 44, 46, 54, 57ff, 70ff, 82, 86-87, 88, 91,

Khrushchev, Nikita S. (*continued*) 93, 101, 102, 104, 112, 130, 132; and "secret speech" (February, 1956), 26, 106; visits Camp David (1959), 70-71

Kipling, Rudyard, 95

Kirghizia (Union Republic), 28

Kirov Ballet, 41

Komsomolskaya Pravda (Communist Youth newspaper), 81

Korean war, 98

Kosygin, Aleksei N., 12, 35, 79, 132

Kremlin, 21, 23, 26, 32, 33, 36ff, 40, 45, 49, 53, 56, 87, 93, 104, 106, 112, 113

Latin America, 94, 114, 116. *See also* Cuba

Latvia (Union Republic), 28, 29

Lenin, Vladimir Ilyich: belief in concentrated authority, 27; comes into power, 16ff, 125; construction of Socialist Order, 18; death of, 20, 21, 35; fails to de-

Lenin, Vladimir Ilyich
(*continued*)
fine Communism, 20;
references to, 5, 14,
19, 52, 79, 82, 93;
sets up Communist
party, 21, 31
Leningrad, 11, 17, 35. *See
also* Petrograd; St.
Petersburg
Lermontov, Mikhail, 89
Liberman, Yevsey, 78
Libermanism, 78-79
Lithuania (Union Repub-
lic), 28, 29
Lomonosov, Mikhail, 64
Lumumba, Patrice, 118
Lvov, Prince, 17

Malenkov, Georgi M., 32,
36, 37
Manchuria, 97, 98, 100
Mao Tse-tung, 98, 101, 104,
134
Marx, Karl, 18, 19, 20, 50-
51, 52, 60, 72, 80, 93,
99
Matzkevich, V., 55
Mayakovsky, Vladimir, 90
Mendeleev, Dmitri, 64
Middle East, 12, 47. *See
also* Asia; India
Mikoyan, Anastas I., 34

Miller, Arthur, 90
Moiseyev Ballet, 41
Moldavia (Union Republic),
28
Molotov, Vyacheslav M.,
32, 36, 37
Mongol invasion of Russia,
7-8, 13, 24, 104. *See
also* Genghis Khan
Mongolia, 112, 128; Outer,
96, 101-2
Mongolian People's Repub-
lic, 102
Moscow, 5, 6, 11, 12, 14,
15, 25, 27, 28, 37, 42,
47, 48, 58, 67, 77,
103ff, 119, 132. *See
also* Kremlin
Moskvich (Russian auto-
mobile), 76
Mussorgsky, Modeste P.,
89

Nasser, Gamal Abdul, 108
NATO. *See* North Atlantic
Treaty Organization
Nazis, 3, 86
Neizvestny, Ernst, 91
Nekrasov, Viktor, 88
New Zealand, 60
Nicholas I, Czar of Russia,
22
Nijinsky, Vaslav, 89

North Atlantic Treaty Organization (NATO), 123-34
North Korean Communist party, 112
Novy Mir (magazine), 90

Okudzhava, Bulat, 87

Paustovsky, Konstantin, 90
Pavlov, Ivan, 64
Pavlova, Anna, 89
Peking. *See* Communist China
Peter the Great, 6, 7, 15, 64, 133-34
Petrograd (now Leningrad), 17
Poland, 59-60; polycentric tendencies in, 110; uprisings of 1956, 109
Politburo. *See* Communist party: Presidium
Pravda (newspaper), 26-27, 82
Presidium. *See under* Communist party
Priestley, J. B., 90
Pushkin, Aleksandr S., 89

Rimsky-Korsakov, Nikolai, 89
Roosevelt, Franklin D., 29

Rumania, 108; polycentric tendencies in, 110
Russia: abolition of economic regions in, 77; agricultural advances, 10-11, 71, 74-75; agricultural backwardness, 9-10, 52ff; agricultural production, 54-55; alcohol problems and restrictions, 85; anti-Semitism in, 88, 92-93, 111; arms and tank production, 8; automobile industry, 6, 8, 18, 76; capital-goods industries, 11, 70; chemical industry, 64; clothing, 6, 11; coal production, 62, 63; collective farming, 9, 21, 45, 52ff; and Communist China, 80, 95-105, 107ff, 125ff; consciousness of European heritage, 126-27; consumer goods, increase in, 43, 70, 75-76, 79; conversion to industrial state, 5, 9-10; creative arts in, 86ff; cultural backwardness, 9; dairy production, 54-55; defense spending, 11; delinquency in, 86; eco-

Russia (*continued*)

nomic development, 9, 52, 63ff, 72-80 *passim;* educational system, 38ff, 44; electric power. 63; financial difficulties, 11; five-year plans. 64, 68; food shortages. 6-7, 9, 10-11, 56ff; foreign aid, 11, 59; future of, 122ff; gas production, 69; governmental system, 18, 24, 27ff, 47ff, 65; highways, 7; holidays in, 26; housing shortages, 6, 8, 11; Imperial, 62; industrialization, 5, 9-10, 64-80 *passim,* 116; Iron Curtain, 23; iron ore production, 63; labor productivity, 6; living standards, 6, 9. 11, 12, 42ff, 51-52; meat production, 54-55; metal-processing industries, 64; military academies, 15; military capacity, 5, 8-10; national divisions, 28-29; natural resources. 6, 62ff; new class in, 45ff; nuclear power, 5. 7, 67-68; pig-iron production, 62; political

Russia (*continued*)

backwardness, 9; political balance, 26-27. 131; political intrigue. 36; population, 6; post-Khrushchev, 6, 77-78. 104; post-Stalin, 13. 15-16, 30, 40ff, 89 (*see also* Khrushchev, Nikita S.); post-World War I, 5; post-World War II, 4-5, 15, 67-68. 123; press, changing, 43; racial problems, 118-19; religions, 91ff; rocket power, 5, 6, 68; scientists, 7, 8, 46, 64; shopping in, 6; size, 6; Soviet-American relations, 127, 130; space race, 6, 7, 11, 34, 46-47, 48, 68; standards of living, 6, 9, 11, 12. 42ff, 51-52; steel production, 8, 11, 62-80 *passim;* sugar production, 63, 64; support of India, 113; technological power, 9, 48, 68; textile industry, 63, 64; tractors, manufacture of, 63; universities, 64; working conditions, 6; younger generation in. 81, 94, 118

Russian Baptist Church, 92

Russian Orthodox Church, 6, 91-92, 93

Russian Republic (Union Republic, 28

Russian Revolution (1917), 4, 16ff, 61, 64, 117, 125. *See also* Bolsheviks; Lenin, Vladimir Ilyich

Rykov, Major, 4-5, 9, 42

St. Petersburg (now Leningrad), 15, 17

Salinger, J. D., 90

Saroyan, William, 90

Scriabin, Aleksandr, 89

"Scythians, The" (poem), 127

SEATO. *See* Southeast Asia Treaty Organization

Shostakovich, Dmitri, 87

Siberia, 10, 17, 99, 105; slave labor in, 15-16, 22, 66

Sinkiang Province, China, 98, 100

Southeast Asia Treaty Organization, 124

Soviet Central Asia, 101

Sputniks, 68

Stakhanovites, 65

Stalin, Josef: anti-Jewish purge conducted by, 93;

Stalin, Josef (*continued*) builds "Communism in one country," 21; builds Siberian slave-labor empire, 15-16, 22; and censorship of citizens, 21; death of, 10, 13, 23, 32, 36, 107; denounced by Khrushchev, 26, 39, 42, 106; drive to industrialize Russia, 10, 21; eliminates kulaks, 21, 53; enforces collectivization, 21, 59; and industrial purges, 67; launches first five-year plan, 64; lowers Iron Curtain, 23; portrait of, 25-26; *references to,* 5, 23, 30, 33, 35-36, 40, 44, 46, 53, 68, 69, 70, 86, 89, 97, 104, 127, 132, 133; and restrictions on foreigners, 21; and secret police, 16, 21, 41, 43; seeks to oust Mao Tsetung, 98; and suppression of the arts, 89-90; tyranny under, 31-32

"Stalin's Heirs" (poem), 86

State Planning Commission, 74

Stravinsky, Igor, 89

Supreme Soviet (Russian parliament), 28, 30

Suslov, Mikhail A., 112

Tadjikistan (Union Republic), 28

Tchaikovsky, Pyotr Ilyich, 89

Tennessee Valley Authority, 20

Tito, Josip Broz, 44-45, 107, 108

Togliatti, Palmiro, 106-7, 110

Tolkachi (expediters), 72-73

Tolstoy, Leo, 89

Trans-Siberian Railroad, 96

Trotsky, Leon, 17, 21, 35, 52

Turgenev, Ivan, 82, 89

Turkmenia (Union Republic), 28

Tvardovsky, Aleksandr, 89

Ukraine (Union Republic), 3, 28-29, 54, 75; revival of anti-Semitism in, 92-93

Union Republics, Soviet, 28-29

United Nations, 29

United Nations Relief and Rehabilitation Agency, 61

United States: admired by Russian youths, 81ff; agricultural comparisons with Russia, 55; easing of Soviet-American tensions, 130; foreign aid program, 47, 59; and North Vietnam, 114; nuclear weapons production, 67-68; opposes Bolsheviks, 20; references to, 6, 10-11, 18, 30-31, 42, 63, 69, 71, 98-99, 118, 124; Soviet-American relations, future of, 127

Updike, John, 90

Uzbekistan (Union Republic), 28, 29

Vietnam, 115, 129; North, 114

Volga (Russian automobile), 76

Volga River region, 15, 52

Voznesensky, Andrei, 87

West Germany, 130-31

World War I, 5, 17, 29, 103

World War II, 3-4, 9, 15, 23, 29, 58, 61, 67, 68, 83, 86, 98, 122, 127

Yashin, Aleksandr, 87
Yevtushenko, Yevgeny, 86,
    87, 88, 92
Young Communist move-
    ment, 92. *See also* Rus-
    sia: younger generation
    in

Yugoslav Communist party,
    44, 45, 59
Yugoslavia, 108

Zhukov, Georgi K., 32, 33,
    35, 37
Zinoviev, Grigori Evseye-
    vich, 35

HARRISON E. SALISBURY

Harrison E. Salisbury has been with *The New York Times* since 1949, and was made an assistant managing editor in September, 1964. Before becoming a news executive, Mr. Salisbury had made an outstanding name for himself as a reporter and foreign correspondent, especially on Soviet affairs. In 1955, for his distinguished reporting from the Soviet Union, he won a Pulitzer Prize for International Reporting. After joining *The Times* in 1949 Mr. Salisbury served as its Moscow correspondent until 1954, when he returned to the New York staff. In the years that followed he covered a wide range of reporting assignments in the United States and abroad. In 1959 and again in 1961-62 Mr. Salisbury revisited the Soviet Union and traveled extensively in the Soviet Far East, Siberia, Central Asia and Mongolia.

Mr. Salisbury was born in Minneapolis, Minnesota, and is a graduate of the University of Minnesota. He worked in the United Press bureaus in Chicago, Washington and New York and became London manager for U.P. in 1943. He went to Moscow for U.P. in 1944 and was U.P. foreign news editor from 1944 to 1948. His books on the Soviet Union include *Russia on the Way, American in Russia, To Moscow—and Beyond, Moscow Journal* and *A New Russia?* His novel, *The Northern Palmyra Affair,* is set in the Soviet Union. Mr. Salisbury is also the author of *The Shook-Up Generation,* a study of adolescent delinquency.